GITCHIE

The Survivor's Inside Story of the Mass Murders that Shocked the Heartland

Phil Hamman & Sandy Hamman

eLectio Publishing

Little Elm, TX

www.eLectioPublishing.com

Gitchie Girl: The Survivor's Inside Story of the Mass Murders that Shocked the Heartland
By Phil Hamman & Sandy Hamman

Copyright 2016 by Phil Hamman & Sandy Hamman
Cover Design by eLectio Publishing

ISBN-13: 978-1-63213-200-0
Published by eLectio Publishing, LLC
Little Elm, Texas
http://www.eLectioPublishing.com

Printed in the United States of America

5 4 3 2 1 eLP 21 20 19 18 17 16

The eLectio Publishing editing team is comprised of: Christine LePorte, Lori Draft, Sheldon James, Court Dudek, and Jim Eccles.

Without limiting the rights under copyright reserved above, no part of this publication may be reproduced, stored in or introduced into a retrieval system, or transmitted, in any form, or by any means (electronic, mechanical, photocopying, recording, or otherwise), without the prior written permission of both the copyright owner and the above publisher of this book.

If you purchased this book without a cover, you should be aware that this book is stolen property. It was reported as "unsold and destroyed" to the publisher and neither the author nor the publisher has received any payment for the "stripped book."

The scanning, uploading, and distribution of this book via the Internet or via any other means without the permission of the publisher is illegal and punishable by law. Please purchase only authorized electronic editions, and do not participate in or encourage electronic piracy of copyrighted materials. Your support of the author's rights is appreciated.

Publisher's Note
The publisher does not have any control over and does not assume any responsibility for author or third-party websites or their content.

To Roger, Mike, Stew, Dana, and their families.
God's peace be with you.

Acknowledgments

First and foremost, a special thank-you to Sandra for having the courage to share this story.

We also owe a debt of gratitude to: everyone at eLectio Publishing, as their tireless work has been exemplary; Amy Schmidt, Sioux City East High English teacher for her editing; Jodie Hoogendoorn, editor at the *Lyon County Reporter* for digging through archived newspaper photos; the staff at the Lyon County Clerk of Courts for allowing us access to boxes full of legal documents; Sheriff Stewart Vanderstoop, Tom Vinson, son of former Sheriff Craig Vinson, and former Deputy LeRoy Griesse, who all gave valuable insight not only into the crime but also into the personalities of individuals we portray; LeLand Baade for contributing memories about his brothers, Stew and Dana, and their parents; and also Lynette Hadrath Dahl for providing details about her brother, Mike.

Additionally, several people helped to create dialogue as it would have been when exact conversations could not be recalled. Our sincere thanks to the family members of the boys, as many memories were painful to relive. Some family members shared but wished to remain anonymous. Through this story we aimed to portray the heinousness of the crimes while at the same time honoring the memory of four admirable boys.

Phil and Sandy Hamman

It has long been a dream of mine to tell the inside story of that night at Gitchie Manitou, but for years this desire was overshadowed by the emotional trauma that resulted in forty years of silence on my part. I can now rejoice that the truth has been recorded and any misinformation from the past can be laid to rest so my family, especially the grandchildren, and my friends can understand the full impact of that tragic night. I thank Phil and Sandy Hamman for making this dream a reality. Thank you to Mary Roche, a victim's advocate who worked tirelessly for a year and a half arranging the prison visit at Fort Madison, where the staff, especially Warden Nick Ludwick, graciously allowed me the opportunity to help heal an old wound. I left your facility feeling like a different person. My gratitude to Kevin Kunkel for filming the event. Mary Maddox, my rock at Fort Madison, and Debbie Fogelman, my two real-life angels whose friendship and support has endured even through agony and heartbreak. My life is better for the many friends and family who gave their support over the years, including my mom for always loving me and being there for me, my caring husband since 1986 who is the most selfless person I know, my niece Chelsea for always sticking up for me, my Lakota cousin for his patient teaching of the Native ways, all my family including the Cheskeys and Rousseaus. You are all very important to me.

Sandra Cheskey Chrans

CONTENTS

Chapter 1
November 18, 1973

"Everyone who does evil hates the light, and will not come into the light for fear his deeds will be exposed."

John 3:20 (NIV)

Had it been a movie, dark notes from a lone violin would have begun playing as soon as the man glanced away from the road to watch his wife, who was applying her frosted lipstick while gazing into the visor mirror. The eerie tempo would have intensified when he shimmied the wheel to test its stability while cruising down a county road breathing in the smell of new leather, first turning the air and then the heat on and off. Both worked, everything felt just right, and they were almost sure they'd buy this car. He checked his watch to see if there was still time to continue the test drive through Gitchie Manitou for one last look at the fall colors before returning this perfect ride.

Gitchie Manitou State Preserve in Lyon County is located in the most extreme northwest corner of Iowa, just a few miles southeast of Sioux Falls, South Dakota. He turned off at the entrance to the ninety-one-acre preserve, and the whir of new wheels on blacktop switched to the familiar sound of crunching gravel. Here the dramatic music would have grown more suspenseful. A rabbit darted across the road, and off to the right a whitetail deer stood in waist-high yellow prairie grass warily watching the car. He hadn't driven but fifty yards further when something up ahead alongside the road caught his attention.

"What's that?" He turned to his wife. They knew this area well, and whatever was up there was definitely out of place among the rustic landscape. The man eased the car to a stop, stepped out leaving the door hanging open, called to his wife to stay in the car, and walked curiously toward the strange objects in the grass, thinking it couldn't possibly be what he thought it was. In this split

1

second, the perfect morning deteriorated into one of the most horrific days of his life.

This can't be happening. It's not real. How could this be? Each explanation was as preposterous as the one before. The music would have reached its climax. Sprawled on the ground before him were three human figures, the arms and legs stiff and still and contorted into grotesque shapes. The bodies bore witness to what had obviously been a gory and unforgiving crime. The gaping wounds that riddled their bodies oozed dried streaks of glutinous blood. Tissue and blood splatters sprayed the dying brown grasses that cushioned the lifeless shapes. For a moment, the man glanced at the open eyes of the corpses who lay before him. Their fixed stares pleaded for someone to reveal the truth behind what caused their gruesome ending. The man raced back to the car and sped to the nearest phone.

Craig Vinson, a no-nonsense lawman with a serious disposition, worked long hours as the Lyon County Sheriff in this sparsely populated corner of Iowa. Anyone who thought the life of a rural sheriff involved handing out speeding tickets and having coffee at the local diner had no idea about the domestic abuse and physical trauma he witnessed on a regular basis. The worst calls were highway fatalities, the senseless carnage reminding him of life's fragility. Now, after a demanding week that included an elusive theft ring that had escaped apprehension, he was looking forward to this day off, which he intended to spend in front of the television watching his favorite team, the Chicago Bears, even though he wasn't entirely confident they could pull one off against the Detroit Lions. The interruption of a phone ringing came as no surprise, having a large social circle in the small town of Rock Rapids, Iowa.

However, this phone call was not a social one. Chuckling, he hung up the phone and asked his wife, "Can you believe it? Someone called in a report about three dead bodies over in Gitchie Manitou. Might be those darn rookies over in the next county

2

getting back at me with one of their pranks!" Several regional sheriffs and police officers in the surrounding counties had a good rapport with each other which led to frequent incidents of good-natured antics that sometimes crossed the line of good taste. Vinson hoped to be back by the time the football game started. His attention to duty prevailed and within minutes he was headed toward the state preserve. Could be some teenagers up to their horseplay. He envisioned pulling up to the park to find three people passed out after a night of drinking or some straw scarecrows covered in fake blood set out by kids with nothing better to do than try to frighten innocent park-goers. Vinson was a natural at detective work, and he was already mulling over all the possible outcomes for this situation in his head. "And for this I'm working on my one day off," he muttered to himself.

Vinson pulled into Gitchie Manitou while surveying the surroundings and managing to stay centered on the one-lane road, which consisted of two narrow gravel grooves for the tires and a grass center in between. Not far from the entrance he pulled up by three still figures lying in a field of brownish-golden grasses. Vinson immediately realized this was much worse than any prank thought up by some reckless teenagers. He removed his hat, shook his head, then took a deep breath before letting out a sigh; all thoughts of the Chicago Bears vanished. He mumbled some words of disbelief, then, careful not to disturb the crime scene, squatted down near one of the bodies. He collected his thoughts and switched seamlessly into detective mode.

Before the hour had passed, crime scene tape criss-crossed the park entrance, and his one deputy, LeRoy Griesse, was preparing to search for clues. Competent as well as genial, Griesse was a boon to the sheriff's department. While the business of constantly dealing with criminals can cause some in law enforcement to become hard-nosed or calloused, Griesse had managed to retain his warmth and compassion along with a sense of justice. He enjoyed meeting the people of Lyon County and was known to greet any familiar face with a hearty, "How have you been?" When duty called, though, he just as easily shifted into the role of diligent detective.

At the moment, Vinson was on the police radio calling for a crime-scene photographer. "And get a hold of the Sioux Falls Police Department as well. We're going to need all the help we can get with this one," he notified the dispatcher.

The muffled shouts of Deputy Griesse calling his name off in the distance drew Vinson's attention. The urgency in his deputy's voice left no doubt that something serious was at hand, yet the sheriff had no idea that the day was about to get considerably worse.

Chapter 2

With silky, flowing, brown hair and vivid chestnut-colored eyes, thirteen-year-old Sandra Cheskey had what her friends considered the good fortune of frequently being mistaken for a much older teenager. She was the youngest of four, and her mother, Delores, or Lolo as friends called her, was responsible for both the French and Cheyenne River Sioux genes that contributed to Sandra's beauty. In her younger days, Lolo had caught the attention of many men herself until Cameron, a young man with good looks and a lean build, came along. Not wanting to lose his prize, Cameron showed up with a ring after just a few months of dating and drove Lolo to the courthouse, where they were married that morning.

Five children followed in quick succession, but her second, a baby boy, died shortly after birth. The doting nun at the small Catholic hospital showed the baby to Lolo before quickly scurrying the lifeless bundle out of the room. Exhausted and shocked from losing her newborn, it didn't occur to Lolo at the time to ask to hold her baby, and the anguish she felt from that decision followed her for the rest of her life. At the time, she could not imagine a worse pain for a mother.

Soon, two more boys followed, and when Lolo went into labor with Sandra, she nearly lost her, too. Lolo was staying with relatives in the remote town of Eagle Butte, South Dakota, when the contractions came suddenly. As luck would have it, the only person around was a neighbor with little driving experience. While the neighbor lady careened down isolated roads to the nearest hospital, Lolo gritted her teeth and clenched the seat to suppress screams of pain, fearing she'd distract the lady and cause her to drive off the road. That wasn't the biggest problem, however. Having delivered four previous babies, her labor progressed quickly, and Sandra made her entrance in the back seat of the car. The inexperienced driver was so focused on the road that she didn't realize Lolo had given birth until Sandra announced her arrival with the screams of a healthy baby. Perhaps this unusual birth foreshadowed a life that would be equally remarkable.

As the years went by, financial stress along with the strain of raising four children led to more frequent bickering between Lolo and Cameron. The marriage didn't last, and Lolo eventually found herself with three rambunctious boys and one little girl who adored her older brothers, Bob, Jim, and Bill. Four of them vying for their mother's limited time left Sandra craving for attention Lolo couldn't always provide. In addition to working long hours, Lolo had returned to school to become a nurse. So it was decided that it would be best for everyone if the children went to live with their Cheskey grandparents for a time. The children would end up staying there from the time Sandra was eighteen months old until she was almost four. She and her brothers loved this farmstead with the cracked and weathered white paint peeling from the house and a slumping old barn where Sandra and her brothers played, made up games, and developed a love for animals.

It wasn't easy for these aging grandparents to care for the children on a farm where the only modern convenience was electricity, as there was no telephone or running water, but they did it without ever complaining. On Sundays the children awoke to the sweet aroma of homemade cinnamon rolls that Grandma baked before sunrise. Sandra would watch the slice of butter slowly melt down the edges of the soft roll before breaking off small pieces of the warm pastry and enjoying every bite of the fluffy treat which she washed down with a glass of fresh, cold milk.

On weekdays, Grandma washed clothes in a wringer washer, and Sandra would hand her wooden clothespins when it was time to hang them on the line. Every morning she braided Sandra's hair, insisting the little girl look neat and presentable, then made everyone a hot breakfast of cinnamon-sugar toast and oatmeal. The boys helped with small chores, and all of them spent as much time as they could outdoors.

Her grandpa would often lift Sandra onto his lap whenever there was work to be done using the faded green John Deere tractor.

He was grateful for the company after so much solitary farm work, and Grandma was grateful for the break from chasing a preschooler. Grandpa would fire up the old beast of a tractor until it chugged to life and lurched them forward with puffs of black smoke billowing from the vertical exhaust pipe. She would wait on the metal seat while he filled the tractor next to a big gas tank in the yard.

"There won't be a single cow escaping once we're done checking this fence," he said as they bounced along, stopping occasionally to fix a wooden post or a stretch of rusty barbed-wire.

Sandra, who jumped from bed every morning and ran to the window to get a glimpse of the farm animals she considered her "pets," worried that one of the placid cows might end up lost or hurt. Her grandparents marveled at her awareness of animals at such a young age.

"When I'm big I'll bring all the hurt animals here. I'll put them in the barn. I'll make them all better."

Grandpa nodded.

Sandra was brought up attending a Christian church, but with her Native bloodlines she was also raised to respect the circle of life and the great power that keeps the entire universe in balance. The call to do good and believe in good things was a constant presence in her family. At the table, they always sat with folded hands before the meal was served. "Dear God, we pray for those who are homeless and for the well-being of those who are sick or weak. We ask for the wisdom to care for these animals in our charge and for the protection of us all." *And for all the animals everywhere,* she thought, knowing that someday she would bring all the hurt animals she could find to this place of peace and beauty.

Grandpa didn't have any hobbies or spend any time relaxing except for late in the evening. He collapsed in his favorite chair each night, and Sandra would climb up on his lap. She wasn't aware of the aged changes occurring in his body since he performed the difficult farm work without complaint. "Sandra, did you save any animals today?" He was truly interested and not just indulging her childhood obsession.

She nodded seriously. "Three worms and one grasshopper. They were lost in the grass so I put them in the garden by a big flower."

"You're a kind girl. God did good with you."

He was right. Even when she wasn't completely good, she was never too naughty. She'd never even been spanked. She occasionally took advantage of being not only the youngest but the only girl as well. Especially on bath night. Grandma would fill a big galvanized tub with hot water from the stove. The tub was in the kitchen, the warmest spot, and Sandra got the first bath. She would take her time sudsing and playing until Grandma would finally pick her up out of the tub in exasperation. Each brother to follow was left with colder and dirtier water than the one before. Then snug in her pajamas, Sandra would take off in search of Grandpa, who would of course be in his chair, and crawl onto his lap.

The happy, hard-working life continued without a problem except that the children rarely got to see Lolo. They were up at dawn, had become proficient in their little chores, had plenty to eat, and plenty of love to go around, which allowed them to focus on what they did have rather than what they didn't have, which was also plenty. Before Sandra turned four, she and her brothers were able to rejoin Lolo in a nearby town, and a few months later, Grandma sent word that Grandpa had died in his sleep, sitting up in his favorite chair.

The four children spent hours together entertaining themselves since Lolo had earned a two-year nursing degree and worked long hours before returning home to an evening of keeping up a household. She didn't earn nearly as much as a registered nurse and with four kids and loans to pay the family qualified for some government assistance. Each month Lolo would pile the kids into the car, and they'd go together to pick up a box of commodities, usually containing things they loved like cheese and peanut butter.

She could have picked up the food on her way home but wanted them to know where it came from.

"I'm so grateful for this food," she'd remind them each month. This focus on thankfulness would stick with Sandra and be a key to helping her deal with future struggles. There were few complaints from Lolo no matter what life threw her way. She didn't judge people, she tried to understand them, and all her children absorbed this philosophy.

At Christmas Lolo made a trip to the local fire station with the four kids in tow bundled in their winter wear, clean but a little too snug. The air was buzzing with childhood expectations as they waited excitedly in line to receive a present. "Merry Christmas!" a spirited fireman eagerly greeted them before handing Sandra a doll and each of her brothers a truck. Though amazed by the gifts, none of them needed prompting to say thank you, which gave Lolo warm satisfaction. When they got home, one of the boys hurried the others into a bedroom and shut the door. "We don't have anything for Mom. She's not going to get a single present!" So they huddled together on the floor around a piece of paper and made her a card. That night the family passed the time singing Christmas carols, eating hot tuna casserole, and reflecting on the excitement of getting these unexpected gifts. While the boys whooped and hollered around her, Sandra escaped to a quiet corner with her new doll, where she spent the night playing nurse and fixing her doll's imaginary broken bones with toothpick splints she'd taped onto the legs.

With Lolo working long hours, the children took on responsibilities at an earlier age than most of their peers and learned to depend on each other. Wherever Bill was, Sandra was close behind. The kids were unaware of their dearth of material possessions so this had no effect on their happiness. Her brothers were boys to the core and proficient at their mischief, frequently harassing Sandra with various pranks. One night she went into her bedroom and reached for the dangling pull string to turn on the overhead light. Instead of the pull string she felt something squishy and hairy in her grasp and let loose a marathon of shrill screams. Lolo screamed as loud as Sandra, but it was directed at the boys when she found out they had tied a dead mouse to the light cord.

Family was so important that the strong bonds between Grandma Cheskey and her grandchildren sustained time and distance. When Sandra and her brothers returned for a visit, they took to the farm as if they'd never left it. The farm had remained untouched by most modern conveniences. It still lacked indoor plumbing, and the children quickly adapted to making the jaunt out to the weathered-wood outhouse with its stacks of Sears catalogs perched on the bench seat next to the obligatory hole. It was too dark and cold to stumble out there at night, so Grandma gave each of them a large juice can to use instead. In the mornings, they were responsible for dumping the contents of the can into the hole in the outhouse, which Sandra would do immediately upon rising. Her brothers weren't as consistent though, and Grandma would regularly find an undumped can in a bedroom upstairs.

"It's not mine!" her brothers would all claim, and with Sandra being the youngest, Grandma always believed the boys and assumed her little granddaughter had simply forgotten. Out she'd walk holding one of her brothers' cans with her arms stretched out in front of her as far as she could and pouting all the way while they tried to silence their teasing laughter. They loved Sandra, but she quickly learned how to match their playful scheming. The farm left Sandra with memories of love that would empower her in times of hopelessness.

TOP LEFT: Sandra developed a love for animals at an early age. She and brother Bob with their raccoons, Spitfire and Rascal, in 1967.

TOP RIGHT: Even at age 7, Sandra liked dressing in girly outfits.

CENTER: The old Cheskey farmstead.

BOTTOM: After the fire station Christmas party. Jim, Bill, Sandra, and Bob each got a free toy.

1971-1972

By the time Sandra started school, Lolo had found a new man to share her life. As the years went by with all of them under one roof, the stress of four children began to cause problems. Sandra's brother Bill, longing for the independence typical of someone on the cusp of teenhood, especially despised this new man in their lives. "You're not our dad, you son of a bitch! I hate you!" he would scream. The fighting became a daily ritual that upset Sandra deeply even though this new man mostly ignored her.

Years of friction came to a head one day when Sandra arrived home to find that she and Bill were being sent to live with separate foster families. She was confused. A relative said it was because the kids were not minding the adults and that there was underage drinking. Sandra hadn't been drinking, and she wasn't a discipline problem. The only thing she could think of was this new man was not able to deal with all of the children.

Sandra was whisked into the home of a foster family. But not for long. She sobbed into the phone recounting for Lolo how the foster parents had severely beaten their own child with a wire coat hanger. Lolo made arrangements for Sandra to be removed. It was a short-lived relief. Within days Sandra arrived at the doorstep of a second foster family yet held her head high, supported by the empowering words of her father, "You're going to be my little Miss America someday!" It was one of the few memories she retained of him. But the distant words turned powerless in the hands of this cold, uncaring foster family. The family members rarely talked to or even acknowledged her. She felt more like an unpaid hired hand than a child.

"I miss my friends," she'd complain softly to her mom on the phone. "Plus they make me do all their work. I have to get up before dawn, do their laundry, and paint buildings."

"This will be better for you in the end," her mom explained.

Sandra hugged her pillow tightly at night and occasionally hot tears would join her muffled sobs. She'd been torn from her friends, her family, her school. She felt like an intruder, like an insect they'd just as soon swat away if it weren't for all the back-breaking chores she did for them. But Sandra was persistent. She tried to believe the family meant well as her mom had assured her. Still, she kept needling away at her mom during their weekly calls, relaying both subtle hints as well as desperate cries for help. She knew her mom missed her as well, and Lolo finally relented.

"Okay," Lolo sighed one day when she could no longer resist her daughter's pleas.

Sandra squealed into the phone then lifted her hands high in the air while doing a little victory dance under the disapproving eye of her foster mom. Bill was allowed to come back soon also, and Sandra was waiting at the door to greet him with a sisterly hug. She was grateful that the experience Bill had in foster care had been completely different from her own. He had been placed with a police officer who'd welcomed Bill into his family and helped him with any problems that cropped up.

It was good to be together again. But the joy didn't last. Although Lolo would have allowed her children to stay home, she wasn't the one calling the shots. The new man in her life vetoed the decision. Since the children had Native bloodlines, Sandra and two of her brothers were sent to an Indian boarding school.

This shamefully weather-beaten school, located in a sparsely populated area of South Dakota, contained an assortment of Native American students who'd brought with them the psychological baggage that can result from living on the "Rez," a term used for the reservation where they had endured poverty and hardships on par with that of a third-world country. Sandra found herself in this Mission school that loomed over the open South Dakota prairie with its aged brick buildings and curls of paint peeling from the wood trim. She slept in a large dorm room with several other girls. The cots and bunk beds were lined up along walls painted a drab green color. The girls shared a common toilet and shower area with little privacy. There never seemed to be enough hot water for showering, so Sandra often had to endure a miserable quick, cool shower. This was especially uncomfortable in winter when the dorm buildings seemed as cold as the barren fields outside. The food was meager except for the one cinnamon roll each girl was allowed to have following Sunday morning church service. Nuns ran this school with strict expectations for good conduct. Sandra tried hard to fit in and follow the rules, but most of the students viewed her as being too white. In spite of her bubbly spirit and natural ability to make friends quickly, she soon became a target and an outcast.

It wasn't long before Sandra encountered her first bully there. Each morning began with the ringing of a bell announcing wake-up. A dorm rule required a neatly made bed for inspection prior to breakfast. For days this mean girl had been stealthily tearing the covers off Sandra's bed. One morning, the girl openly tore Sandra's bed apart the moment it was made. Sandra pursed her lips together and without a word made the bed again, giving the girl a threatening look. When finished, she stood and faced the girl, fists ready at her side, her sense of justice stubbornly refusing to let this act go unchallenged. The girl smirked, then pushed past Sandra and again ripped the covers off with a few hard jerks. A screaming brawl erupted, and the girls went flying into one of the portable lockers that stood between each set of bunk beds, sending it crashing to the floor. When the fight ended, Sandra stood shaking, but only on the inside, fearing she'd now have her first experience with the "Circle of Discipline." During this almost daily occurrence, students from one dorm would stand in a circle around the offender who had to confess her infraction, at which point a nun would break through the circle and begin whipping the student with a leather belt. In this case, the nuns ferreted out the truth, and Sandra was only required to stand in the circle and confess her wrongdoing to a group of students from her grade.

The other girl admitted her violation then braced herself bravely for what would happen next.

A stern nun lashed the girl's rear several times. She held in her tears, not giving satisfaction to the nun or the other kids intensely watching for weakness. It had been a close call for Sandra though. The strain of constantly watching her back along with the demoralizing atmosphere gradually dampened her bubbly spirit.

At night, atop a thin, lumpy mattress that smelled of must and old urine, Sandra curled herself into a tight ball and fell asleep trying to remember every detail of her friends back home: how they'd laughed, how two friends would each hold one end of a long rope while the third girl jumped, all of them singing a catchy rhyming song about "Cinderella dressed in yella." And how they were all kind to one another. Had the plastic handles of the jump rope been blue? No, green, she remembered, and one handle had a crack that would pinch your skin if you didn't hold it just right. This attention to detail helped her focus on something besides the fact that it was still over a month until she could go back home for Christmas.

Sandra was able to avoid the Circle of Discipline, although the fear of it loomed heavily. Her gut ached every time the belt cracked against another child's thin pants with a slap and a whoosh even when it was someone who'd been less than kind to her. Her gentle heart couldn't stomach the fear and injustice. The cold stares and taunts of "white girl" followed her every day while she sat in a colorless classroom surrounded by jeering whispers and constant ridicule. She met each insult with a brave face, and in quiet moments daydreamed about the shocked looks they'd have on their faces one day when she received her Miss America crown on television as the audience applauded wildly in the background. She knew it was unlikely to ever happen, but she held onto these dreams, one of the only things that hadn't already been taken from her.

What she felt wasn't anger, it wasn't animosity; it was overwhelming loneliness, especially since only sporadic phone calls home were allowed. Sandra waited, counting the days until she'd see her mom again. She marked off each day in her head until there were only two left. Once home, she planned on badgering, explaining, and pestering until she could convince her mom to take her back. But then, the day before Christmas break, she found out the bad news.

"You're not going home," a stern nun explained when Sandra inquired about a bag or suitcase for her belongings. Sandra didn't have much at the school but intended to take it all since she had no plans of returning. The next day, some of the students left to spend Christmas at home while others stayed. Sandra never found out why she was a part of the latter group.

There was little to do around the boarding school during the break. She slipped into a blue fog, with each day stretching endlessly. After the break ended and everyone returned from their homes, life continued on in its own dismal and disconcerting way. The only thing Sandra knew was that she had to persuade her mom to let her come home once and for all.

When the school term finally ended and Sandra and her brothers did get to go home, Lolo was waiting for them at the front door. Sandra raced past the others, throwing her arms around her mother. "My baby girl," Lolo whispered over and over, stroking Sandra's hair. Neither had to say how much she'd missed the other. With a simple touch, the bond between mother and daughter was once again sealed.

Over the summer, Sandra pleaded with her mother, who adored her only daughter. Sandra's well-worded complaints finally convinced her mother not to send her back to the Mission boarding school. Sandra was relieved; her boarding school nightmare was finally over. The family was back together. The fighting in the house had calmed down. It looked as if the worst was behind them.

Sandra and her brothers had settled into a comfortable summer routine of lazy afternoons at the nearby swimming pool and neighborhood games of kick-the-can at night. She was close with her friends, and all of them were looking forward to starting eighth grade that fall at the junior high, which was within walking distance of Sandra's house. Life was finally good again.

Then out of nowhere, Lolo gathered the children to inform them that due to a job change they would be moving from Minnesota to a tiny town in South Dakota. The kids had never heard of Tea, South Dakota. Despite well-worded protests—none of them wanted to get sent away for causing a problem—the moving van was packed and they were on their way. The children, now in their teens, except for Sandra who would turn thirteen in a couple of months, were crushed over leaving familiar friends.

Chapter 3
Summer 1973

The family settled into a large farmhouse outside the small town of Tea, South Dakota. Sandra and her brothers often walked the half mile into town for something to do throughout the remainder of the summer. Sandra quickly met several friends, including a girl named Debbie who lived just down the road. Even though Debbie was three years older than Sandra, the two were drawn to each other through their love of animals, music, and watching movies. Debbie had a sister as well and sometimes, due to the proximity of their houses, the three girls all hung out together with Sandra's brothers. They were a bubbly group and would spend hours together talking, laughing, and making batch after batch of Kool-Aid to quench their thirst in the hot, waning days of summer.

One Friday night before Sandra started school in nearby Harrisburg, she was watching *The Brady Bunch* while sitting cross-legged on the couch with a bowl of buttered popcorn on her lap that she was eating one piece at a time. The television was cranked up louder than necessary, as it usually was, to account for the noise that came from having a houseful of kids.

Ring ring. "I've got it!" she yelled, jumping off the couch and half dropping the popcorn bowl onto the coffee table, where it spun nearly to the edge. "It's for me," she yelled again before answering the phone. If one of her brothers answered, they would jokingly hold the phone out of her reach or say something embarrassing to the person on the other end before giving her the phone.

"Hey, Debbie!" It was her good friend who lived down the road, and the two talked every day.

"You're watching *The Brady Bunch,* aren't you?" she asked.

Sandra laughed. "Yes, so why did you call now?"

"I knew you'd be home! Listen to this song. I just heard it for the first time this morning." Debbie held the receiver to the radio and turned up the volume so Sandra could hear it.

"I heard that song this morning, too! My brother kept turning the volume up really loud and when I'd tell him to turn it down, he'd turn it down so far I couldn't hear it!" They both laughed while Sandra tried to stretch the phone cord from the kitchen far enough into the living room to grab her popcorn before one of her brothers took it. The cord was so twisted and kinked that she nearly pulled it loose, all because she didn't want to set the phone down and interrupt Debbie.

"Please go to the Starlight with me tomorrow, Sandra. It won't be fun without you." The Starlight was a drive-in movie theater in the nearby city of Sioux Falls that was a popular summer attraction where kids hung out with friends or went to meet new ones. Sandra hesitated just slightly. There really was nothing better to do, but she barely had enough money to go.

"Pleeeeease. I never meet boys unless you're with." Debbie laughed again. It was true. Besides her exotic French-Indian features, Sandra had skin that glowed satiny tan, especially so when amplified by the summer sun. She possessed curves that could pass for a high school student, which attracted the stares of many boys and the jealousy of many girls. The attention never went to her head. In fact, she often seemed oblivious to their boasting and swaggering, having observed the actions of her brothers over the years when girls were around. So far, the adoration of her father, who had said that Sandra was going to be his little Miss America some day, had sufficed. Yet recently she found that she didn't mind the attention heaped on her by some of the boys when she and Debbie would walk into town. Sandra no longer threw her hair into a ponytail before departing on these walks; instead, she now kept a comb handy so her hair could flow freely about her shoulders while she and Debbie chattered their way into town.

The following evening was hot but clear, typical for the time of year and just right for a night at the Starlight Drive-in Theater. The girls sat in the car but not for long. The whole purpose of coming here was to socialize, not watch movies. The soundtrack was blaring through the metal speaker attached to the door of the rolled down window, and the smell of fresh popcorn and chili dogs hung in the air. Sandra gazed down the rows of cars, some with children sitting on blankets atop the roof and others surrounded by small groups of teenagers laughing and sipping ice cold Cokes or whatever illegal beverage they might have sneaked in.

"Let's go," Debbie said, eager to see who else was there.

Sandra wore a delicate summery top with flowing sleeves and cut-off jeans. Her flip-flops caught bits of gravel with every step.

The concession stand was in a sparse cement block building crammed with an impatient crowd waiting to get back to their cars and friends. The two girls stood in line, but then some people who Sandra didn't know motioned for Debbie to join them. When Sandra went to leave the concession stand ten minutes later with a pack of licorice, she'd lost sight of Debbie.

Sandra stepped from the stuffy building into the mild night. Not twenty feet away and headed straight toward her was the most handsome boy she'd ever seen. The world blurred and glimmered, becoming a vacuum containing only Sandra and this suave boy with layered black hair flowing in the breeze, as if she'd been transported into a movie. A hint of a smile crossed his face when their eyes met, sending a quiver skipping through her. The boy walked right up to her. Later that night, and for days—no, years—to come, she'd replay the moment over and over with eyes closed and an irrepressible smile on her face. She'd think of how it had been almost like those too-romantic-to-believe moments portrayed on made for TV movies designed to appeal to women, but it was more than that because even the most talented author or brilliant movie producer can't capture the emotion that sweeps through a young girl on the cusp of first love. All the overused platitudes whipstitched together couldn't describe what she felt: *her heart stopped; she literally froze in her tracks; their eyes met; it was love at first sight.* She didn't just see Roger for the first time. She felt him clear through to her soul. And suddenly, there he was in front of her.

"Well, hello," he said assuredly as if they were old friends. The warmth of his eyes glinted with serenity as though they were kindred spirits. He extended his hand. "I'm Roger Essem. What's your name?"

Sandra tucked a piece of hair behind her ear, reached out after a brief pause, bowed her head just a bit, and shook his hand. "Sandra Cheskey," she replied softly.

They fell into an easy conversation, and she found out that Roger was a student at Washington High in Sioux Falls. He was with his good friend Stewart Baade. Sandra purposely avoided the topic of school, only mentioning that her school was in Harrisburg near the town of Tea. They talked for about fifteen minutes before Roger asked for her number. "I'll call you, and maybe we could do something together."

Though inexperienced in the art of flirtation, Sandra walked away elated.

"Where did you go?" Debbie asked, throwing her hands in the air when Sandra reappeared later on.

"Didn't you SEE him? Oh, Debbie, he was so confident, not like most boys who don't know what to say. And he is gorgeous, I mean SO gorgeous. He's going to call me, and you HAVE to meet him." Then she regretted saying that. Would he call? As a hopeful teenage girl, she couldn't get Roger off her mind all night. She kept hoping he'd happen to walk by their car, but he didn't.

The next day, Sandra replayed the previous night over and over. Why hadn't she found out more about him? Why hadn't she walked around more? Maybe she would have run into him again. He'd probably lost her number. The day dragged on, and just when Sandra plopped onto the couch to read a book, the phone rang.

"I've got it! It's for me!" she yelled at the top of her lungs. She raced to the phone with hopeful anticipation.

It was Roger, and they talked for nearly an hour. When the conversation ended, it was with the words Sandra had been aching to hear. "Do you want to go to a movie with me next weekend?"

Late Summer 1973

Roger and his friend would be there to pick her up at five o'clock. Sandra started getting ready by mid-afternoon. In a bathroom filled with clouds of steam that sent rivulets of water sliding down the wall, Sandra was oblivious to the sound of one of her brothers banging on the door with muffled shouts to hurry up. She shampooed her hair for the second time and picked at a hangnail, which in its waterlogged state pulled back too far and began to bleed. She huffed then washed off the blood before carefully examining her legs and using the soapy razor to remove any stray hairs she'd missed the first time. This was followed by a careful application of make-up and a bout with the blow dryer to attain the perfectly silky locks that could only be achieved in this humidity by careful attention to the application of the various hair products spread along the bathroom sink.

Just after five, Roger's friend Stewart, or Stew, pulled his old blue van into the long drive in front of the house. Roger hopped out wearing a plaid coat that Sandra thought was a perfect match for his lean, muscular build. He walked Sandra to the car and opened the door for her. *A true gentleman, like in the movies.* Her stomach quivered, and she suppressed the smile spreading across her face so she didn't appear too pleased. She was mature enough not to have unrealistic expectations of being pampered like a princess but definitely expected respect from any boy who intended to hold her interest.

They sat toward the back of the State Theater, first Sandra, then Roger, and finally Stew. There in the darkened room Roger reached over and held her hand. The movie was *Night of the Living Dead*, which gave Sandra plenty of excuses to squeeze Roger's hand and lean in close to him. When he walked her to the door later that night, he gave her a gentle hug but their lips never met. Not that night. Sandra fell asleep with sweet thoughts of their perfect first date.

Regular dates followed. Roger continued to treat her respectfully and demonstrated maturity beyond his years—something he and Sandra had in common. Stew, because he had a vehicle, accompanied them on these dates. When Roger finally kissed her, it was during a walk through Falls Park in Sioux Falls next to the roaring water of the Big Sioux River. It was a quick kiss on the lips, but it was enough to cause a change in Sandra. Something magical happened the moment their lips met.

When Roger again walked her to the door that night, she felt a small, unwelcome shudder in her stomach. There was something she had to tell him, and she wasn't sure how he'd respond. Once he knew, there was a good chance he wouldn't want to see her again. She'd been meaning to tell him since the night they'd met, but the time never seemed right. He deserved to know, but she couldn't bring herself to do it now. Not after the perfect kiss. Not after this perfect date. Life was too good to ruin it by telling him.

Chapter 4
November 18, 1973, Morning

Sheriff Vinson signed off with the dispatcher and hurried in the direction of his deputy's shouts, making mental notes along the way: the entrance to the park was blocked off, several officers had arrived from the surrounding area, and more were on the way to assist with a thorough search. He reminded himself to tell the officers who would be assisting to bring extra crime scene tape for this large area. His job as sheriff had yet to require the supplies needed to investigate a murder of this magnitude. Had it not been for the three dead bodies sprawled along the road, it would have been a perfect day for a walk through Gitchie Manitou, an untouched nature preserve whose name literally means "Great Spirit," the name given to the great creator by the Anishinaabe Indians. Nature had adorned the park with smooth pink outcroppings of bedrock that formed natural steps and ledges for hiking among the three hundred plant species of the area. Each season brought forth a new show of prairie flowers, and the last of the asters had already faded away during the frigid fall nights.

A slight wind sent soft flutters through the golden prairie grasses and the scurrying of small birds and animals here and there broke the otherwise peaceful silence of the surroundings. The specter of death dampened the natural beauty, and Vinson had to fight off the impulse to imagine the sounds of agony that must have filled the air as one body after another fell to the ground. Even the sweet aroma of fall leaves, crisp beneath his feet, took on a stifling odor that permeated Vinson's mouth and nose.

He rounded the edge of an old camp shelter, its eight-foot-high walls constructed of purplish quartz block sections probably quarried not far from Falls Park. The weather had been crisp, and the ground was hard. There were no footprints or tire tracks visible to the eye. The remains of a cold campfire stood at the side. Vinson started to piece together a crime scene adjacent to a glowing fire further down the path. He began to envision not how the scene looked at the moment but how it had appeared during the throes of the homicides. To Vinson, crime scenes were three dimensional, and he noticed not only what he saw but how the layout made him feel as well.

In the short time he'd been here, he'd noted that a steady stream of South Dakota troopers, crime-scene photographers, and officers from the Sioux Falls Police Department had begun to arrive. By the end of the week this would unfold into a massive investigation by eight law enforcement agencies from South Dakota and Iowa. There were acres of land to comb, and Vinson knew from experience that cases like this either wrapped up quickly, with clues left by a careless criminal and a quick arrest, or lingered on, requiring volumes of manpower.

"Hey, Vinson." It was Deputy Griesse yelling with a troubled voice. "They found another body."

Vinson swiftly moved to the area. Beneath the drooping, leafless branches lay another still figure. He removed his hat and ran his hand over his head, then took the notepad from his pocket and began to write.

Male. Mid-teens. Black hair. Plaid coat.

He shook his head and let his hands drop to his sides, the pages of the notepad fluttering in a wind that was slowly gaining speed. He turned to the deputy, and the two of them said almost in unison, "What happened out here?"

Chapter 5
November 16-17, 1973

Washington High School in Sioux Falls, South Dakota, is a massive four-story building with expansive windows that allow natural light to stream in. It is constructed of Sioux quartzite, a durable stone that resists erosion and contributes to the beautiful rock formations in and around the Big Sioux River near Falls Park. It is the same stone that is used by Plains Indians to carve ceremonial pipes and can be found in buildings all around the city and surrounding area. In the 1970s, around 2,100 tenth-to twelfth-grade students attended this school each year.

Roger Essem's friend, Mike Hadrath, lived half a block away from Roger so the two spent much of their time together both at and away from Washington High. Mike was a popular sophomore with a ready smile. What set him apart from others was his unparalleled athleticism; tall, lean, and muscular, he was a tenacious competitor who was a starter on every team. In basketball he consistently led in points scored. He pitched all spring and summer in baseball, leading one team to the Little League regional championship tournament. His PE uniform shorts were adorned with multiple President's Physical Fitness Award patches, the hallmark of a well-rounded athlete. Even as a sixth grade student at Franklin Elementary he'd set a record of forty-four pull-ups. After twenty years, longtime PE teacher Judy Jasper reluctantly retired his record since students had given up trying to beat it and remarked, "Here's a kid who not only had athletic ability but worked hard to set records and never caused a single discipline problem."

Mike's accomplishments along with his refreshing modesty drew him into a popular social circle. His good friend Roger Essem loved music and classic cars, but what drew others to Roger were his quiet ways and genuine interest in their lives. Throngs of

Washington High students of all grade levels considered Roger and Mike to be their friends.

On a Friday afternoon in mid-November, the two crossed paths in the crowded hall and made plans for the weekend. Leaning against their lockers and amid frequent interruptions by their peers to "have-a-good-weekend-see-you-on-Monday," they decided to invite some friends to trek out to Gitchie Manitou State Preserve where they could build a fire, shoot the breeze, and play some music. Since Stew had a van he would drive.

Mike came from a close-knit family with parents who adored their children and felt that having meals together and sharing conversation was important. Mike looked up to his older brother, also a standout athlete, and he doted over his little sister. Mike helped her with whatever she needed and had just taken her trick-or-treating a couple weeks prior.

The next day, in typical Mike style, he kissed his mom goodbye. Stew and his fourteen-year-old brother, Dana, would be here soon to pick him up to head to the State Preserve. She watched Mike swing his way through the backyard on the clothesline pole as he headed to the alley behind their house to wait for Stew's van.

Chapter 6
November 17, 1973 2:00 PM

At 2:00 PM on Saturday afternoon, Sandra was brushing her hair in front of the mirror, counting the strokes so that she brushed long enough to get a glossy shine but not so long that it looked greasy. She couldn't stop thinking about Roger's smile and the way he'd tenderly stroked her hair last weekend before once again giving her a small kiss on the mouth. He treated her and looked at her in a way that was exciting and romantic. The phone rang.

"Don't answer it! It's for me!" her brother yelled from the next room in a girly voice, clearly attempting to sound like Sandra and not bothering to move from his spot on the couch in front of the blaring television. Sandra smiled and leapt for the phone.

She made a face at him and rolled her eyes at his spot-on impression of her then picked up the phone.

It was Roger. "What are you doing tonight?"

Her heart jumped and a small smile spread across her face. "Why are you asking?"

"Well, Stew and Dana are coming to my house, and we're planning on going out to Gitchie Manitou. I was wondering if you wanted to come along." As soon as he'd asked, Roger regretted that he hadn't asked her sooner. Because it was the weekend, he assumed she already had plans with some girls down the road from her with whom she'd recently become close friends. Stew and Dana were more of the laid-back, easygoing musician types who went with the flow of the moment when it came to making plans. In fact, that was how the whole night had come together. The boys thought it sounded really "rock-n-roll" to spend an evening in front of a fall campfire singing into the night and playing their music.

"Sure," Sandra replied. "If someone will come out and get me. Maybe Stew will. Do ya think so?"

"Yeah, he will 'cause I really wanna see you." Roger had already checked with Stew, who was such a good friend he was willing to drive twelve miles out of the way to pick up Sandra and then another fifteen miles to Gitchie Manitou. Roger finally allowed a smile to cross his face. He adored Sandra and regularly marveled at his good fortune of meeting her that night at the drive-in theater. They were a perfect match, and now he'd be able to spend the rest of the day with her.

"I wanna see you, too. When ya coming?"

"Right now!"

Sandra's mom worked long hours late into the evening, which left Sandra with more liberal hours than most girls her age. She'd always been responsible, though, and often had three older brothers looking over her shoulder. This newfound freedom in the hands of a girl gripped with young love was too irresistible. When Roger called, she melted.

By the time 8:00 PM rolled around, Sandra had started to worry. Really worry. Maybe Roger had changed his mind about doing something with her. Maybe Stew didn't want to drive all the way out to her house. She tried not to keep glancing at the phone but found herself willing it to ring so she could at least hear Roger explain why he hadn't come to get her. She kicked off her shoes, turned on the television, and curled up on the couch clutching a pillow. *I will not cry. I will not cry.*

Brrrrinng! Sandra jumped from the couch, almost tripping over her bare feet.

"Hello!" she said breathlessly.

It was Stew. "Sandra, we're coming pretty soon, but we had to make some stops."

Sandra nodded into the phone and bit her lower lip. "You know, my brother just got home, would you mind if he came with?" Sandra and Bill had been through so much together that they relied on each other for friendship as well as emotional support. They watched out for each other, and both included the other in their circle of friends. He was about the same age as Roger and his friends.

Thirty minutes later Stew's battered blue van pulled into the drive. Naturally outgoing, Sandra emerged from the house exuberant to be spending the evening talking and laughing, two of her favorite things. Roger opened the door for her, and she climbed in. Bill was just about to get in the van too when his best friend pulled into the driveway. "Hey, Bill! I'm going to a party and that hot chick you like will be there."

Bill looked at Sandra sheepishly, but she laughed and waved him off. "Go see the girl! I'll talk to you tomorrow." Though she was totally at ease with Roger, something felt off as soon as she set foot in the van. Perhaps leaving so late at night seemed odd to Sandra. She was younger, though, and decided it probably wasn't out of the ordinary for teenage boys to be starting their plans so late. Roger stroked her hand, and even in the bumpiness of the van, it seemed as tender as usual. But something was out of place. Sandra noticed then that it wasn't just the four of them; there was another boy sitting in the far back.

"Who's that?" she asked Roger quietly.

"That's Mike. You met him before," he said, turning around to Mike. "Hey, Mike, this is Sandra. Sandra, this is Mike." That was another quality she adored about Roger. He was comfortable around everyone and so considerate of her. He didn't hesitate to introduce her to another of his friends. Then she recognized Mike.

"Oh, hi, so you were the one that was in here when Stew gave me a ride home from the show, right?"

"Yeah, that was me," Mike said, smiling. The van was mostly dark, but she could see flashes of Mike's face every time they passed under a street light. His arms were folded in front of him, and he nodded his head slightly to the beat of the music coming from the radio in front. At that moment Mike didn't strike Sandra as being anything other than one of Roger's friends. She knew of him from her conversations with Roger, but there were many things she didn't know about Mike's background and personality. She definitely had no idea at that moment that some of the decisions he'd make that night would change her life forever.

Chapter 7
November 18, 1973 Mid-morning

Several somber investigators gathered around Sheriff Vinson, who stood just outside the bright yellow crime scene tape that sealed the entrance into Gitchie Manitou. With the job at hand falling on his shoulders, his mind focused on several scenarios at once. He helped establish a chain of command, taking one of the lead roles. His eyes scanned from the road into the park, down to the natural stone ledges that blocked any further view. He began delegating tasks to his team. On site were two veteran detectives from the Sioux Falls Police Department. Both were specially trained and would bring more foundation to the Iowa group. They conversed about the immediate evaluation of the crime scene, then began a systematic process to gather evidence.

Of special concern was the location of the fourth victim. Iowa troopers had discovered his body by rocks and a tree near the campfire. This was near the imaginary line that divides the South Dakota portion of the park from the Iowa side. It was of vital importance to know in which state this murder had occurred in order to determine where charges would be filed once the perpetrator was caught. A surveyor was called in to locate the exact boundary lines. Later that day he informed the officers that the victim had been killed just a few yards inside the Iowa line.

As the various lawmen began to do their jobs, Vinson gave them some final advice. "Gentlemen, this is a high-profile case. Make sure every step you take while continuing inside that tape works to our advantage and preserves evidence." And Vinson was right. The sensational case soon made headlines across the nation. The experienced team was unaware that a strange twist would occur later in the day which would be their key to eventually solving the case.

Chapter 8
November 17, 1973 9:00 PM

Roger held Sandra's hand as the van careened down the highway. Occasionally the two would find themselves just leaning against each other in comfortable silence. When the van came to an unexpected stop, Sandra realized they were nowhere near a park. They were back in Sioux Falls.

"Where are we?" she asked Roger, who didn't seem at all bothered by this unexpected turn of events.

"Oh, Stew's going back to get his guitar."

That seemed reasonable, and after Stew returned with a guitar case, they drove for some time until they reached the thickly wooded area of Gitchie Manitou. Dark had nearly settled and the looming silence along with dim shadows of skeletal trees and scrubby bushes unnerved Sandra. She reached for Roger's hand, and he pulled her close.

"Is anyone else out here?" she asked, trying to sound curious rather than frightened.

"I don't see any cars. I don't think so," Stew answered. Everyone unloaded from the van except Dana, who was leaning in the side door rummaging for paper to start a campfire. While Roger surveyed the area with Sandra, Stew moved closer to the camp shelter to find a good place to build their fire. He was glad he'd worn his warmer coat and zipped it to the top, kicking away leaves with the toe of his shoe here and there to uncover small twigs for kindling. The park was filled with small night sounds, the low roar of the river beyond the campsite, an occasional scamper, and just a small rattle of wind in the mostly barren bushes.

"Hey, Roger!" Stew called over his shoulder with an edge of concern in his voice. "Come look at this!" Stew was crouched before a fireplace in the camp shelter nearest the road. They'd come to a shelter with a fire pit surrounded by walls made of aged quartz block criss-crossed with yellowed vines that had dropped their leaves, lending the appearance of a medieval castle. Stew's back was to the others, and he was poking at something in the fire pit.

Roger hurried over and saw that it was an abandoned campfire. "The coals from that fire are still red, so someone must have been here," Stew said, somewhat apprehensive. Concerned that this area had already been taken, they moved farther down until they were near the soaring bank of the river.

An autumn chill had descended, necessitating the warmth of a fire. Roger and Sandra returned from the tree line and added their armloads of dead wood onto the growing pile. Stew, using the paper Dana had found, soon had a roaring fire. The flames licked their way into the black night, and the growing fog inhaled the pleats of smoke. Roger pulled Sandra closer. She leaned her head against the warm fabric of his plaid coat.

Dana perched himself on one of the felled logs near the fire and prepared to throw on more wood, but a sinister sound in the distance stopped him. His eyes were pulled to the dark trees beyond the shelter. He stood slowly.

"Did you guys hear something?"

Chapter 9
November 17, 1973 5:00 PM

Dana Baade was a soft-spoken and well-liked eighth grade student at Patrick Henry Junior High School in Sioux Falls. He had every intention of following in his big brother Stew's footsteps to become part of the next great American band. Both brothers loved music, and Dana would practice strumming his brother's beloved guitar whenever it wasn't in Stew's hands. Dana was quiet, reserved, and good-natured. He often waited for Stew to speak up for both of them when the situation required it. Although the two brothers had their spats, they relied on each other for support and defended each other loyally when needed. Dana admired Stew for many reasons. Stew was responsible and balanced a part-time job at UPS while still in high school, managing to save enough money to buy his own van. Openly generous, he readily gave rides to whoever needed one. The brothers had visions of forming a rock band with Stew playing guitar and Dana on bass, which he aspired to learn.

"Teach me another chord," Dana would beg Stew, who usually dropped what he was doing to demonstrate the finger movements for his little brother. Neither had the opportunity to take music lessons so had to depend on others and their natural ability to learn the craft they were honing with their shared guitar.

A song with a particularly loud guitar solo came on the radio and Dana cranked it up, playing along to the music and trying to match the notes with what he actually knew how to play. In his mind, though, he was on stage wearing low-slung blue jeans and a faded T-shirt, whipping his long hair, which he washed and brushed tangle-free every day, back and forth. The song ended and Dana turned the volume down a little so he could try out some of the new chords he'd been learning. It didn't sound half as good without the radio blaring in the background. He set the guitar back in the corner of the bedroom and went off to find his warmest coat. He'd have to ask for Stew's help with that chord tomorrow. Tonight he was going to Gitchie Manitou with his brother and some friends.

Chapter 10
November 17, 1973 9:50 PM

Dana wasn't the only one who'd heard the strange sound. Roger immediately turned away, preventing Sandra from seeing the concern on his face, but she heard it in his voice. "Stew, don't play the guitar, and everyone be quiet for a minute." His voice was serious.

Sandra thought she heard a twig snap nearby, and when she saw Roger's head jerk in the direction of the noise, it confirmed what she already knew. Much later, she'd wonder how the human ear can be so perceptive that even in the woods on a dark night, it can discern the difference between the sound of an animal stepping on a twig as opposed to that of a human. *Crunch.* Pause. *Crunch.*

Snap! Another twig. No one could ignore it this time. The sound was much too close.

"What was that noise? Do you think someone's out there?" Dana asked, worried that they'd intruded on someone's camping ground who was now coming back to reclaim their spot.

"Yeah, I keep hearing leaves crunching," Sandra said, glad that she wasn't the only one who was concerned.

Roger pulled her closer to him. "Listen." His eyes looked serious, which made Sandra uneasy. She'd never seen this look on his face or heard the worry she'd gleaned from the one word he'd quietly uttered. "It could be a bear." Roger tried to lighten the situation. Stew nodded, although all of them knew there were no bears in the area.

The five of them stood wordlessly around the fire, which flickered and hissed, sending sparks of light into the silent darkness. Roger wracked his brain trying to remember where he'd heard the same snapping and cracking in the past. *It has to be an animal, right?* His main concern was Sandra, though. What if it wasn't an animal? He'd defend Sandra without hesitation.

Mike's athletic instincts kicked in at the sound of the next unexpected noise. He was competitive, and no matter what was out there, Mike wouldn't go down without a fight. There was a hot tingle in the back of his neck, the same feeling he got when someone passed him the ball with ten seconds left and his team was down by two points. The same feeling he'd had pitching the last inning of a game when the crowd was screaming and it was up to him to make sure the batter struck out. Mike loved the competition. He didn't rattle easily, but something didn't feel right. He pulled the collar of his brown corduroy jacket up around his neck and stood with one foot slightly back, ready to spring into action if needed.

Chapter 11
November 18, 1973 Late morning

With a keen eye trained to detect a ghost of a tire tread or the smallest bullet fragment, the crime scene photographer stepped gingerly among the orange flags that marked potential evidence for the case. He angled his rapidly clicking camera to avoid the dappled shade cast by the gentle sway of thick branches on nearly barren trees in order to accurately capture details the detectives would use to reconstruct the crime scene.

Several yards away, a coroner was conducting a visual examination of each body, writing detailed notes that included observations of blood flow patterns and the location of each wound. Without disturbing the body that lay before him, he squatted down and leaned in, noticing that the victim's coat had rolls and bunches consistent with having been dragged.

After the investigative team finished up their extensive search of the surroundings, they regrouped to share their findings and assessments but with much less evidence than Sheriff Vinson had hoped for. There were shotgun shell casings and an acoustic guitar that had been left leaning against a tree. A search of the bodies yielded not only some identification, but also cash as well. Other than those specific pieces of information, the evidence was lacking any sort of direction.

"Robbery doesn't appear to be the motive at this point, but we can't rule out anything yet. Let's all be thinking of what motive could have been behind this," Vinson instructed the group. Then he contemplated a part of the job that cut the deepest. It was time to inform family members of the victims that their loved ones would never return home again. He glanced at the short list of names; first on the list was the name *Roger Essem*. Also weighing heavily on his mind was the lack of evidence. Enormous pressure from the community to solve this case in short order would surely be expected as soon as the news broke. He'd allot himself little sleep until this case was solved.

Chapter 12
November 19, 1973 2:00 AM

Alone in the pitch-black of the night, Deputy Griesse sat tensely in his patrol car, alert to every outside rattle that in the uncertainty of darkness took on macabre tones. A murky fog was descending onto Gitchie Manitou, enveloping the park with a chilling vapor. He'd been assigned to remain overnight to protect the crime scene until investigators could return at daybreak to wrap up their final searches. Griesse would come to remember this assignment as the most frightening event of his entire law enforcement career.

He had already spent an emotionally exhausting day investigating the gruesome sight of the blood-stained scene and seeing what close-range shotgun blasts had done to maim and disfigure the four teenage boys, their bodies blued and twisted. He hoped that few people would ever see the photographs of these bodies, knowing it would leave lifelong scars on their minds. He tried to shake the macabre images from his head, but they held fast. A murky gloom had cast its hold on the campsite just yards from where the grisly murders had taken place; the specter of death bottled up within the foggy woe. Compounding the fear he felt was a lack of sleep and the fact that the murderer or murderers were still at large. Would they return to the scene again tonight as criminals often do?

His eyes jerked on the brink of exhaustion, causing his mind to play tricks on him. Through a sleepy stare he thought he caught movement at the front of the vehicle, then at the side. Griesse bolted up and flicked on the headlights, but there was only the rolling fog floating over the field where the bodies had lain earlier that day. He stretched his eyes open as far as he could a few times and took some slow, shallow breaths. He fought the temptation to leave the headlights on. That would make him a visible target. He scanned the park relentlessly. Yet again he sensed someone stalking up to the patrol car ready to fire a shotgun blast through the window.

And so the spooky, unnerving images haunted him throughout the night, the ghostly aura refusing to relinquish its grip on the park. It was the longest and most frightening assignment of his life and would cause him sleepless nights for years to come. When the sun finally broke through onto the eastern horizon and light overcame the darkness, Griesse sighed with relief. He had never been happier to see the sun.

Chapter 13
November 17, 1973 10:00 PM

Mike, Roger, and Sandra stood silently around the fire. No one moved; the only sounds piercing the suspense in the air were that of a hooting owl and a light rustle of wind blowing leaves along the ground. To break the tension, Stew grabbed his guitar and strummed a few chords, lightly at first then louder, until everyone soon felt some relief. Stew and Dana sang several songs before taking a break. Stew sat down in front of a hollow tree. Dana and Mike stood next to the fire. Mike's eyes slowly scanned the tree line, but the light from the fire fell dim at that distance so he found himself facing a sea of black. Sandra laid her head on Roger's shoulder, but she didn't fold into his body the way she had when they'd cuddled in the back of Stew's van on the way home from Falls Park last week. Roger's body was rigid, and his left hand was pressed against the log as if he might bolt upright at any moment. After a few tense minutes of quiet, the group relaxed, perhaps a bit embarrassed that they'd frightened so easily.

"I know what we need," one of the boys announced, pulling from his pocket a thin white cigarette rolled tightly at both ends. He inhaled deeply, held his breath, and passed the marijuana to Sandra. She took a small puff and blew it back out, wanting to fit in. As the joint continued circling among the friends, Sandra waited for the marijuana to lift away her fears, but it had the opposite effect instead.

"That fire's dying down. Come with me, and we'll get more wood," Stew said, nudging Dana. Sandra was glad Roger was right next to her on the log. It gave her a small semblance of safety. She tried to block out the eerie sounds and concentrate on the romantic fire, its faltering flames swaying under a starry sky. She breathed in the scent of Roger's coat and warmed herself with thoughts of telling the girls at school on Monday about another perfect date with her handsome boyfriend.

"Show us his picture!" and "Did he kiss you?" one of the girls was bound to say, one of them always did, and then they'd all ooh and aah over Roger and how lucky Sandra was to be his girlfriend. She never tired of the attention heaped on her by her doting friends when they'd eagerly gather around to hear every detail about Roger, how he was such a gentleman. She wished she'd had a camera to bring tonight. She could have had Stew take a picture of her with Roger, his arm protectively around her shoulder, sitting next to a blazing fire. Well, it would be blazing again soon when Stew and Dana got back with more wood. *Why weren't they back yet?* She didn't have a photo of her with Roger, and when Sandra made up her mind, she did it with determination. She'd borrow a camera. Maybe Debbie had one. Then her thoughts were interrupted by another strange sound. Sandra gasped. By the way Roger and Mike froze at the same moment, she knew they'd heard it, too. The three slowly stood; Roger's arm never left her shoulder.

"It's like they want us to hear them," Mike said, confused by the increasingly loud cracks off to their left. "Stew! Dana! Where are you?"

"Over here!" one of them called back. But it was in the opposite direction of the noises.

Twigs snapping and the bewildering sound of branches brushing against something continued with increasing regularity.

"Now it's like they're on beat. Like someone's walking." Roger said aloud what they were all thinking. The sound edged closer each time. Roger turned just in time to see Stew and Dana burst through the darkness. Their arms were nearly empty as neither had found much wood dry enough for a fire.

"Hey, man, something's going on. There's someone out there." A tinge of alarm had crept into Roger's voice. All five teens once again scoured the edges of the campsite, the once roaring fire now glowing weakly, illuminating just a small area around the campsite. What happened next put a chain of events into action. Although all five of them sensed something was off, they had no idea the night was about to take a terrifying turn.

Chapter 14
November 17, 1973 10:00 PM

Deputy Griesse poured the last of the steaming coffee into a tall mug balanced on the dash of the unmarked vehicle and settled back into the seat with a sigh. The night was turning frigid, and the car needed to remain hidden to avoid detection. Lyon County, nestled in a picturesque corner of Iowa, struggled with the same crimes and social problems as the rest of the country, just on a smaller scale. This evening, in fact, marked the third night of a stakeout. Griesse was parked on a gravel road near a farmhouse where the two occupants were prime suspects in a series of thefts. Vinson was parked two miles away near a spot where the suspects were thought to be stashing the stolen items. The officers communicated by radio and were focused on catching the thieves in possession of some items stolen just that day. The deputy lifted binoculars to his eyes each time car lights pierced the darkness, but they were mostly useless now. A heavy fog had rolled in and was growing thicker.

"The farm is dead tonight," he reported to Vinson, knowing that catching the bad guy involved a lot more time sitting in the dark for endless stretches than most people realized.

"Nothing here either."

"Is it foggy over by you, too?"

It was, and Vinson knew that signaled a close to the stakeout. Another evening with nothing to show, but that's how it went in this business. "Well, we'll wrap it up for tonight then. We should probably take a trip through Gitchie Manitou and see if there's a beer party to break up," Vinson said.

Griesse eased onto the road and headed in the direction of the park. Teenagers regularly gathered in the three-walled camp shelter for a night of beer drinking in what they perceived to be a remote location where their adolescent adventures would go unnoticed. He and Vinson often chased away as many as fifty kids in one night.

After he'd traveled less than a mile, the road dipped, engulfing the patrol car in a thick fog. Griesse stepped on the brake and flipped the fog lights on.

"We've got pea soup over here," the deputy reported into the radio, peering out the window on his side of the car. "I can't even see the edge of the road."

"I'll head away from the river and see if I can drive out of this cloud. It is thick."

But the fog had unfolded itself across a wide berth, and Gitchie was still several miles away from both men. Dedication to duty was a hard habit to break, though, and their constituents valued a clean county, so Vinson and Griesse made regular weekend trips through Gitchie to prevent the park from acquiring a less than savory reputation as a party place. Both men tried a few different routes to the park and, after one had a near head-on collision in the dense fog, made the mutual decision to head home after a long day. They both switched directions and steered their patrol cars away from Gitchie Manitou, where, unbeknownst to them, five teenagers sat around a campfire wondering what was making strange sounds in the woods surrounding them.

Chapter 15
November 17, 1973 10:30 PM

Roger's and Sandra's eyes caught the distant movement at the same time. Roger dropped his arm from her shoulder and took a few strides forward, keeping Sandra back at a safe distance.

"Stew! Did you see that? Two guys just ran across over there!" Roger shouted, pointing into the blackened night air. Mike, Stew, and Dana all whipped their heads around in the direction Roger was pointing, but they missed the two large figures that had now disappeared into the night.

"Say something to them!" Stew urged Roger.

"Hey," Roger yelled. But there was no answer, and the sounds of cracking twigs ceased. *Perhaps there were some campers out there who intended to return to this spot.* Minutes passed before the soothing sounds of the flowing river and raccoons emerging from their daytime hideouts to scour for food fell into a peaceful rhythm.

"Let's find some more wood and get this fire going," Roger said, and the others agreed. Roger started to walk away, then turned, grabbed Sandra in a tight embrace, and gave her a soft, lingering kiss comparable to a scene in a movie when a soldier kisses his love for the last time before heading off to war.

"Hey, Roger, do you want me to come with you?" Stew asked.

"Yeah, that would be nice," Roger answered with an even voice. He paused just at the edge of the night where flickering firelight met pitch-black woods. There was movement again in the nearby tree line. Roger stopped and yelled, "Who are you? What do you want?" His question met stark silence followed by the encroaching crumple of leaves. Suddenly, two ominous figures splintered the night atop a low ledge of rock not twenty feet from the teens, with a third shadowy silhouette visible just behind them. They emerged from the darkness, moving methodically. Sandra's muscles clenched in fear at the sight of their scowling faces. Her knees nearly buckled, but she forced herself to remain standing. They held guns; one raised his weapon.

BOOM! A terrifying explosion ripped through the campsite. BOOM! Then another.

Lean and dauntless, years of athletic training enabled Mike to react quickly in the face of adversity. He grabbed Sandra and pulled her along until they reached a sheer drop-off at the river's edge where they shielded themselves behind a tree.

"Stay still," Mike ordered as he held her protectively behind the only barrier that stood between them and gunfire.

Their bodies taut with fear, they waited as quietly as possible, trying to suppress their loud, panicked breaths. Even in her state of confusion, Sandra's first instinct when Mike grabbed her had been to keep sight of the shooter to stay out of the line of fire. The man holding the shotgun had been tall and had worn a Russian trooper hat with ear flaps that covered most of his short, brown hair. Hot tears strained at the corners of Sandra's eyes, yet her thoughts were consumed with finding Roger, though she didn't dare to move. The gun blast had filled the air at the same moment she'd seen Roger flinch and crumple to the ground. She knew Roger was out there, wounded and helpless, and all alone. She held back the sobs of terror that racked her body and held tightly to Mike. Their soft gasps seemed amplified in the desperate effort to become noiseless and blend in seamlessly with the woods around them. At first there wasn't a sound except for the occasional rattle of leaves tossed by the wind.

Another shot rang out and all went still until the blast's echo dwindled to nothingness. Finally Dana's usual soft-spoken voice broke the stillness. "Stew! What happened?" There was no answer. Then a loud wail rose from the direction where Stew had been.

"I've been shot! They shot me!" Stew's voice was laced with pain and determination.

Sandra yearned to hear Roger yell back, but only Stew's distressing groans filled the night. She turned slowly to Mike to avoid making noise and whispered, "What's going on?"

"I don't know," Mike whispered back.

They could hear Stew several yards away moaning in pain. "It hurts, it hurts so bad..." His voice trailed into silence.

Sandra tried to imagine herself becoming one with the tree. She pressed her face close to the trunk and breathed in the scent of musty bark. The gunmen retained their position of advantage on the ledge, causing snippets of their whispered conversation to reach her. Trembling, she pressed a hand to her pounding chest and prayed the men would leave. Though wanting nothing more than to make it all stop, she forced herself to stay alert. Then the three shadowy figures on the ledge shifted position and turned directly toward her and Mike.

Chapter 16
Early 1970s

The cascading falls of the Big Sioux River had long been a place where people gathered to live and play. This scenic area around Falls Park, where tall quartzite ledges create a series of waterfalls and thundering sprays of water send halos of mist skyward at the base of the turbulent waters, gave Sioux Falls its name in 1856. It was along this river's edge that Roger Essem refined his appreciation and love of nature. He was especially fond of mountains and volcanoes and as a budding artist sketched countless scenes of the outdoors. On the flat plains of South Dakota, he had to settle for roaming small hills, but dreamed of one day visiting the mountains he spent hours sketching. The area around the falls wasn't particularly hilly, but the untouched stone and acres of tall grasses allowed for a full day of hiking along the river's edge, where he sometimes brought artist's paper and charcoal pencils to sit peacefully sketching. He could often be found hiking with friends and taking advantage of the area's varied seasons.

Roger grew up along with his eleven siblings near these flowing waters in this working-class side of town. His parents taught and expected their children to demonstrate respect, so with this humble demeanor he developed an appreciation for nature and life in general. Roger made the best out of everything life had to offer and became known as a people-person who was well-liked in return. Teachers at school respected Roger's willingness to help classmates. His good-natured personality was cultivated as he matured into his teens. "He's the type of person anyone would be honored to have as a son," one teacher quipped. Roger knew he'd always like being around people and would forever have a special connection with the outdoors.

Chapter 17
November 17, 1973 11:00 PM

After what seemed like an eternity, a voice rang out, "We're with the police! Come out with your hands up!"

At first neither of them moved. Mike stiffened when Stew's moans of pain sliced the silence again. "We're with the police! Come out with your hands up," the voice demanded.

"Don't run, those cops have already shot at us," Mike whispered to Sandra while the two confused teens slowly emerged from the thicket, their hands raised high in the air. "There's two of us, don't shoot," Mike yelled to the three assailants shrouded in darkness. As they walked closer to the men, Mike, filled with adrenaline by the situation, asked, "Who the hell do you think you are shooting at us?" The tall man with the Russian hat trained his gun on Mike and without saying a word pulled the trigger. The force of the blast knocked Mike to the ground with a thud. Though not hit herself, Sandra instinctively fell to the ground next to Mike. She was trembling with fear but tried to remain as still as possible.

A sickening pain radiated down Mike's shoulder and warm blood spread through his shirt, then his jacket. He was bleeding and in excruciating pain, yet the hard-nosed athlete did not cry out or beg for his life. He lay as still as Sandra, who in the light of the waning fire could see the faces of the three men, all wielding shotguns. Two were thin and one was chubby, all their shadowy faces appearing menacingly evil in the dim light. A scene from a horror movie where some teenagers were murdered by a crazy, knife-wielding killer flickered through Sandra's mind. *This is what it feels like to be in a nightmare.* She prayed they'd find out this was all a terrible misunderstanding.

Two of the men who'd identified themselves as police talked in hushed voices and moved about the campsite as Mike and Sandra lay silent. One walked over in the direction of Roger. *Maybe they'll think we're dead and leave.* Over and over Sandra prayed for them to walk away. *If they're police, they'll call an ambulance, right?* She wanted to ask Mike the question, but neither dared to even breathe loudly. Then she realized what she'd just thought. *If.* The word *if* hung in the air. *If they were police.* Something didn't feel right. Did police use this kind of force on a handful of teenagers sitting around a fire singing? They weren't in uniform and hadn't shown a badge, but undercover agents wouldn't be in uniform so probably they were telling the truth.

After several moments the men circled back. Mike and Sandra heard the sound of approaching feet. Mike concentrated on slow, calm breaths to take the focus off the pain and weighed every possible option to fight for his life. He too wondered if the men were police. If so, they were the type to shoot first and ask questions later. Mike feared that the smallest movement on his part could yield another gunshot. The closer the footsteps came, the quieter he remained until the rustle-tap of each step came to a stop. Right next to him. He braced himself for what he feared was bound to happen next. *Wham!* One of the men kicked Mike's lower back so hard that his legs skidded forward, and he clutched his shoulder in pain at the jolt of the kick. Spasms gripped his body.

"That one's playing dead!" the other man announced, giving Sandra a swift, hard kick as well. "Get up! Put your hands in the air, and don't try anything!"

In a moment, Mike and Sandra were standing with their hands held high. Sandra's stomach clenched at the thought of the pain Mike was enduring. She couldn't imagine how he'd even managed to stand. She caught a glimpse of someone to her side and saw it was Dana, also with his hands in the air.

They're going to put us in the police car now. Sandra waited to be led to their vehicle and prayed it would be an actual marked police car. Then at least the three of them would know these men were legitimate. One thought hadn't left her mind the entire time. *Where was Roger? Was he wounded like Stew?* But then something strange happened.

"Let's take them this way, Boss," the shorter one said.

"This is a drug raid! Don't make any sudden movements. Do exactly as you're told," the Boss commanded while keeping his gun leveled on the teens. The Boss was the same tall, thin man who had wounded Mike and shot Roger. With the barrel of the gun, he made a sweeping motion to indicate the three should turn around, which created a frightening tension with guns at their backs. *He's going to shoot us in the back! I know he's going to shoot us!* Sandra almost bolted but remembered what Mike had said. *Don't run, or they'll shoot you.*

Instead of leading them in the direction of the road, the Boss pointed to a small dirt path that led further into the woods. "Follow that trail!" he barked.

Their stomachs turned. The three teens had a feeling that whatever was about to happen wasn't good. They were heading deeper into the woods. There was nothing in this direction but cliffs, the river below, and rocky ledges that were nearly unnavigable in the dark night.

Sandra knew Dana to be quiet and obedient, especially around adults, and as of yet he had hardly spoken. She glanced over at Mike. He was pale, sweaty, and Sandra worried he might collapse. Emboldened by Mike's bravery, Sandra forced herself to utter four words. "Okay, please don't shoot!" It was all she could muster, and she hoped it would convey the message that the three would cooperate. She just wanted out of there. *Please, God, get us out of here quickly!*

The Boss herded them down a trail for just a short distance before stopping them on a ledge overlooking the Big Sioux River. Sandra's heart raced. She couldn't move, couldn't dare to look at Dana's or Mike's face in case their expressions revealed that they knew more than she did. She wanted to ask questions. *Where are you taking us? Why did you shoot Roger? He hadn't done anything! And Mike? And Stew? All Mike did was ask a question, and they'd shot him!*

She stood there silently while the Boss briefly conferred with the other man. He was heading back toward them, gun held in front, and Sandra sucked in her breath, hoping he wasn't going to use it again. *Be quiet. Don't say a word.*

"Keep walking! Follow that trail!" he ordered again.

There was no noise except for the sound of feet on dead leaves. Mike was trudging much slower than the others; then his words broke the silence. Sandra startled at the unexpected voice.

"Sir, can we put our hands down?" Mike's voice was strained, which reminded Sandra that he'd been wounded. He wasn't moaning, complaining, or causing any problems. She couldn't fathom how he'd walked this far in his condition.

"Yeah, you can put them down." The Boss's voice was aloof. This concession on his part led Sandra to think he might really be a cop. *If he wasn't a cop, he wouldn't take the chance of letting us put our hands down, right?* Yet it was disturbing that they were being led further into the woods.

Mike's steps behind her became faster until he was next to her side.

"Can you help me walk?" he asked in a low voice.

Sandra wrapped her arms around his waist. He'd been shot on the other arm, so she was careful to place her hands where she wouldn't touch the wound. Being propelled into this role of helper gave her something to concentrate on; she had to be the strong one now. She marveled at the connection she already felt with Mike even though they'd only known each other for a few hours. *When this is all over, the first thing I'll do is kiss Roger and then tell Mike how amazing he was.* Because of Mike's warning, she'd suppressed the impulse to run. Had she bolted it's likely she'd have been gunned down. Sandra forced herself to mimic the way Mike carried on in spite of a gunshot wound to his shoulder.

"Are they really cops?" Dana whispered to Mike.

"I don't know," Mike replied in a steady voice. He likely thought all of them had a better chance of survival by facing the situation head-on rather than giving false hope and convincing themselves these men were cops. He was one to stick to the facts and deal with whatever was at hand.

Then Dana's voice was at her side. "I hope they're cops." She'd heard Dana's voice so seldom, she hardly recognized it. Dana seemed more likely to sing than talk, and the seriousness of his voice concerned her.

Mike walked with his arm around Sandra, leaning into her for support, so she was almost relieved when they were ordered to sit down.

"And don't try anything," the Boss snarled. "There's a guy around the corner."

But his words were less than convincing. There was no corner. There was nothing ahead but more trees, more ridges, and more river. Again, Sandra wanted to ask questions but was afraid of being shot. Mike, however, wasn't about to go down without a fight.

"Are you Mr. Jensen?" The Boss didn't answer. "Well, do you know Mr. Jensen?" Mike's voice was strong and confident. Sandra didn't know who Mr. Jensen was but wondered if it was a ploy by Mike to see if the men were really cops. Again she prayed that the Boss would respond by saying he knew Mr. Jensen, and then they'd all know this whole disaster was at least legitimate and the men were cops. Then a horrible thought made her nearly vomit. Did Mike feel this was his last chance? Was he thinking it didn't matter if he was shot again because the guy was going to finish him off anyway, and he may as well give it a try?

The Boss thought for a moment then answered, "No, I don't know him." Then he turned and walked back toward his partner but remained within eyeshot of the group.

Mike slowly kneeled, then lay down but kept hold of Sandra's hand so tightly it hurt her. She wished she could absorb some of his pain; by nature she was drawn to those with needs or afflictions. She kept her focus on Mike and stayed alert. She rubbed the top of Mike's hand, and her heart sank. Even decades later, she'd marvel at the courage he was able to muster in the face of each successive terror they would encounter throughout the night to come.

Chapter 18

Mike lay motionless on the cold, dirty path. There was only enough light in the night sky to make out the vaguest of shapes. Crumpled leaves clung to his bloody coat, and a heavy fog grew thicker around them. "What do you think they will do?" she asked, certain that Mike's instincts were telling him more than hers.

"I don't know," he replied slowly.

"Try and rest," Dana urged Mike. Sandra wasn't sure if she could see or feel the hopelessness on Dana's face. His voice was steady but...

"Sandra," Mike said, pausing slightly between each word but maintaining a strong front, "I can't feel my arm or move it. Will you put it on my stomach?"

Without hesitation Sandra gingerly lifted his arm, supporting the underside with her hands, and softly placed it on his stomach, which she could feel rising and settling in uneven gasps. The steady beat of approaching footsteps silenced the three teens. Sandra lifted her head and met the gaze of the man the others called the Boss.

"Get up. Keep walking," he bellowed.

Mike struggled to his feet with the help of Sandra and Dana. They walked a short ways down the trail and already Mike had asked twice when the ambulance was coming. Sandra cringed every time Mike spoke, afraid it would provoke the Boss again.

"What are your names?" the Boss asked.

Each, in turn, stated their name. But it seemed to be a desperate diversion on his part. The trail was leading them further into the woods, and there had been no man around the corner. Sandra began to wonder if they should fight back somehow. If they were being led to their death, what could it hurt? Her natural inclination was to relate to people, animals, anything that lived and breathed. If her questions bothered the Boss, well, it was looking more and more like it was just a matter of time before he lost patience with all of them. None of this felt official. It didn't feel right. Sandra mustered up her courage, then spoke.

"Where are we going?" It was a simple question. Non-threatening. And she'd kept her voice steady, not accusing. She allowed herself to breathe again. The Boss didn't answer. She tried again. "Where is Roger? Will I be able to see these guys after you take us in?" She glanced behind her. The gun was pointing straight at her back, yet the Boss remained silent and hadn't told her to shut up, so she pushed a little more. "Will they ride up with me when we go to jail? Will Roger ride up front or is he hurt?" *If he's a cop, he should have answered those questions!*

The Boss snorted. "Absolutely not. That one"—he waved at Mike with the gun—"will be in the prison hospital. You'll think it's heaven compared to where these two are going," he told Mike.

"How long will we get?" Sandra wanted to keep him talking. It felt right. Maybe the Boss was actually warming up to them. She wondered if Mike sensed the same thing or if his thoughts were clouded by pain.

"Five to ten years," he answered after a short pause, a pause that seemed out of place, as if he were searching for an answer rather than responding with something a policeman should know.

"I bet they get ten years, right, J.R.?" the Boss said to the heavy man.

"Yep, ten years," sneered J.R.

"They can't do that! It's our first bust." Sandra almost spun around but caught herself. Before the words were out of her mouth, she imagined Roger behind bars for years while they longed for each other's touch. Then she imagined herself behind bars, too. Alone.

The Boss was closer now, and although Sandra couldn't see his gun she could picture it pointed right at her. "Oh yes they can," he said. "You're in Iowa. The law's harder over here."

"Iowa! How did we get in Iowa?" Mike asked. Gitchie Manitou was just inside the Iowa border, and like many people, Mike didn't realize only a small section lay within South Dakota.

"Well, that's where you are," was all the Boss had to say. He seemed unsure of himself. His actions seemed less and less like that of a policeman with each passing moment. The three of them engaged the Boss in some more conversation before he ordered them to stand still right where they were.

"And don't try anything stupid," he added, then looked around to where two beams of light pierced the woods. "OVER HERE, HATCHET FACE!" the Boss yelled, waving a hand in the air even though it would have been impossible for anyone to see them from a distance. Sandra wondered why he didn't have a police radio in his pocket. The beams of light swayed, stopped, swayed some more, then came to a stop. An engine quieted to an idle before a door opened somewhere in the vicinity of the two lights. "JUST FOLLOW THE TRAIL ROAD!" A muffled response followed, and then the lights gradually grew brighter as a pickup approached. Sandra turned her head to avoid the glare, her arms still tight around Mike's slumping body.

A man with a pockmarked face stepped out of the truck.

"Sir, can we sit?" Mike asked.

"Stand where you are or we'll blow your *&%$#@! heads off!" J.R. ordered.

Sandra saw a look of concern cross Dana's face. She wondered if the words struck him as strange also. *Wouldn't a real policeman let him sit down? He's injured! Maybe not, maybe the police are trained to stay in control.* Confusion mingled with fear, and she breathed slowly to remain calm.

"Is the ambulance on its way?" Mike asked again. The slightest movement racked his body with shocks of pain from the #4 buckshot that had blasted through his shoulder and bicep.

"Yeah, yeah," the Boss said. He seemed rattled by their questions though. "I need your names and ages. Do you have any identification?" The last sentence was punctuated with the tone that if they were unable to produce an ID, it wouldn't be good.

The three men frisked Dana, and one removed a social security card from the boy's wallet.

The heavyset assailant, J.R., grabbed the card from his partner and went over to the headlights to read it before returning it to Dana with a dissatisfied look on his face.

"How many girls are here?"

Dana and Mike both turned to Sandra and said that she was the only one. Sandra's stomach somersaulted, though she didn't know why. Just a reflex, perhaps. *That was a weird question.*

The one the other man had called Hatchet Face told the three kids to sit in a tight circle. "Stay where you are," he added. He was thin also, but shorter than the Boss and had blond hair. He was wearing dirty jeans and a jean jacket buttoned to the top with a heavier coat over it. Then he, the Boss, and J.R. moved back toward the pickup, where they spoke in hushed voices for several minutes.

"I heard them say something about tying our feet and putting us in the truck ," Sandra whispered.

The Boss rummaged around in the pickup before returning to the teenagers with something in his hand. "We don't have the handcuffs with us, so we'll use this." He held up a roll of thin, gray wire.

His eyes locked on Sandra. Facing him now in the fuzzy glow of the headlights, she couldn't deny the evil that sheathed his face. She weighed her options. Running was not possible under the specter of three shotguns. The next time he made her sit down, maybe there'd be a chance to slip away, dart into the trees, and take off into the night.

"Put your hands behind your back." He took a bold step forward and Sandra did as she was told, glancing at Dana and Mike for reassurance. "This will cut the hell out of your hands."

Sandra sensed that he took pleasure in telling her this. *Would a policeman say that?* She wanted to believe that the answer was yes. She was naïve and frightened, and the cunning assailants, either to control her or keep her calm, continued insisting they were police officers.

"Don't put it on so tight." The command rolled from her mouth, and she immediately wondered if she should have a more complacent attitude. The sharp wire had already begun slicing into her skin. Her gut instinct said to fight. Life had taught her how to stand up for herself and not wait for someone else to do it for her. The Boss didn't answer, which felt like a small victory to her.

"Get in the pickup." His voice sounded smaller.

"I can't." She forced confidence into her voice to carry the message that he should have realized she couldn't climb into the high seat with her hands behind her back.

"Oh-oh, that's right. Your hands," he mumbled, then lifted Sandra off the ground and set her in the cab of the pickup. His face was close to hers now, and she let her eyes bore into his vacant black pupils. Sandra had honed her street sense over the years and was able to convey her feelings of acceptance, disappointment, or in this case, anger with just one hard look. Her confidence rattled the Boss more than she knew.

His eyes landed on a gunny sack bunched up on the floor of the truck.

"I'm gonna tie this bag over your head."

"Why?" She kept her voice steady.

"Because you said you were cold."

"No I didn't. Can't you just put up my hood?" She didn't dare hesitate with an answer, and her voice indicated that he didn't know what he was talking about. The Boss shook his head slightly. He was flustered.

"I-I don't know..." His voice trailed.

Before Sandra could respond, J.R. appeared. "Leave it off her," he said before disappearing behind the pickup.

"Look. I'm gonna try and get you off the hook and out of here before the sheriff gets here." In the moment it had taken J.R. to interrupt them, the Boss managed to recover his thoughts.

"Will you take the wire off my hands, then?"

To her surprise, he agreed.

She turned so he could unwrap the wire. His hands seemed clumsy and inexperienced behind her. Sandra wanted to believe that his explanation made sense. She hoped that he was on her side. She'd do almost anything to avoid being sent to a place like the boarding school or another foster home. If she could avoid charges she could then visit Roger wherever he ended up. Something inside wanted to hold onto that glimmer of hope, but things weren't adding up. She was so confused. There should have been an ambulance, normal handcuffs, police badges, and radios.

"What about Roger? Does he need an ambulance?" She was afraid of the answer she might get but wanted to know the truth.

"He was hit with a tranquilizer gun. He'll be fine. Now don't try anything!" he warned for the umpteenth time before locking the door and slamming it shut. He walked back to his partners, glancing back at Sandra as if to make sure she didn't make a run for it.

Being separated from the boys made her edgy. She hadn't realized how much safer she'd felt being with Mike and Dana and how taking care of Mike had distracted her from the terror surrounding them. Now, alone in the silent pickup, its engine off but the headlights still on, her foot met an empty can on the floorboard, and the clink of it made her jump. She took a deep breath. The Boss had returned and was climbing into the driver's seat. Without a word, he put the truck in gear and took off down the road. Sandra turned, and in the fading light saw Dana, Mike, and Stew walking on the road, with J.R. armed and walking behind them. One of the assailants had forced Stew to get up in spite of his pain and march down the road with the other boys. All three looked over at her with such mournfulness it made her heart ache. She looked around for Roger but couldn't find him. For whatever reason, she locked eyes with Dana as the truck rolled out of the park until the two couldn't see each other anymore. For the rest of her life she'd wonder, if she'd known what was going to happen next, was there anything she could have said to stop it?

Chapter 19

J.R. stood guarding the boys. Soon Hatchet Face drove up in Stew's van. He clicked the headlights of the van on bright, trapping the boys in a small curtain of light. The three teenagers stood obediently along the remote park road, squinting their eyes against the blaring light. Their shadows cast far into the grass and disappeared into the darkness. The cold night air intensified the pain searing through Stew and Mike from the buckshot wounds, yet they stood still along the barren road as they were ordered.

J.R. stepped inside the van, and after a brief conversation the perpetrators determined that they would "shoot the little hippie boy first" since he wasn't wounded, and they didn't want him scampering off. Both men hopped from the vehicle with shotguns in hand. The boys hardly had a chance to know what was going to happen next.

Without hesitation, J.R. raised the gun to his shoulder and took aim at Dana, then pulled the trigger. The gun cracked, and buckshot tore through Dana's jacket, slamming his young body to the ground. Already wounded and paralyzed with the shock of seeing his brother blasted to the ground, Stew could not move. More shots rang out. Before Stew could even turn to face his attacker, he fell into the tall grass. Hatchet Face joined in, firing his weapon at Stew as well.

Mike, weakened from pain and sensing he was next, stood facing his executioners. The shotgun roared its deadly sound into the still night. The talented athlete would never compete again. The crazed J.R., not satisfied, continued to pump several more shots into the fallen boys. A haze of gunpowder smoke drifted upward until it had evaporated into the night sky. When the van finally drove away, the park lay silent.

Hatchet Face drove off in Stew's van with J.R. by his side.

"Where we gonna dump this van?" Hatchet Face asked.

Neither had a plan, so J.R. came up with what seemed to him a good solution right on the spot. "We have to go through Sioux Falls to get to the abandoned house, and our car is in Sioux Falls, so we'll get it and leave this van on a side street somewhere." The two were hopeful that the cops wouldn't find the vehicle for weeks; by then the trail would be cold.

"By the time we all meet back at the abandoned house, he'll have done away with the girl, too. Then all the evidence will be destroyed. This is what you call beating the cops at their own game," Hatchet Face gloated.

At the same time that the two killers were driving through Sioux Falls to ditch the van before heading to the abandoned house, Sandra and the Boss were also en route to that house but took a back way to avoid the city. "I'm looking for the lake, but it's hard to find in the dark," he told Sandra. This confused her. *Why are we going to a lake?*

"I missed it!" He slapped the steering wheel and shook his head. "That was the road where you turn to go to the lake. The gas is low though. Almost empty. I know where I can fill up."

He pulled into a wide farmyard with a rambling two-story white house, then drove around the house, past a barn and behind a building with a large red gas tank that is standard equipment on most farms due to their remote locations and large amounts of fuel required by the machinery. It was painted the same red color as the one on her grandpa's farm years ago.

Sandra glanced at him out of the corners of her eyes with a look that demanded to know what they were doing there.

"I have a key to the gas tank, and I have permission to take gas whenever I want, any time I want. But I have to leave ten dollars." His voice conveyed the message that he'd never be anything less than honest.

Sandra hoped since he'd known exactly how to get to this farm and had a key to the gas tank that he was telling the truth. He'd offered a lot of details, and how could he come up with details like that if he were lying? So she thought of a question to test him.

"How about when you're in other states? Where do you get gas?" She wondered if he could answer that one quickly.

"Oh, I have keys, but not too many," he chuckled to himself. Sandra found this odd; it all seemed so bizarre. The Boss removed his shotgun from the rack in the back window of the pickup, which sent a surge of fear rushing through her. But then he replaced the weapon, rearranged some items in the back of the truck, and ordered Sandra to stay put.

After filling up, he eased down the farm's driveway as if trying not to make noise and then began driving down more dark roads. Even in her perplexed state of mind, Sandra noted everything she could. *A crack in the front windshield on the driver's side. An inspection sticker on the dash. White vinyl bench seat.* The surroundings were harder. *Two-lane blacktop road and fields of picked corn everywhere.* Just when she thought the night couldn't get any more confusing, everything took a terrifying twist.

Chapter 20

For a few more minutes Sandra sat in anxious silence. Then the truck hit a rut in the road, causing her to bounce slightly into the air, and she realized she'd been holding her breath, trying not to make a sound. The Boss broke the silence. "Okay, I'm gonna try to avoid the sheriff because if he sees you, you'll have to go in with the rest of them. Now I told my buddies that I was gonna take you girls out and talk to you because you're too young to get busted."

Sandra nodded slightly. She did not want to get busted, sent away to a detention center or a foster home. She wasn't sure what they did with kids her age. Would she have to testify against Roger and his friends? She wanted to ask but was afraid of the answer. She wanted to see Roger again more than anything. No matter how long he got sent away, she'd wait.

"I thought if I talked to you, you'd promise not to tell what we look like or any of that because I shouldn't be doing you this favor. But I promise if you stick with me one hundred percent that I *will* get you out of this. And promise you won't smoke grass anymore either."

Sandra couldn't put her finger on it, but everything he said almost sounded like what a policeman would say. These guys claimed to be with some kind of special police force, though; she'd gathered that much. It wasn't as if she were in any position to argue or bargain anyway. "I promise. But why did you just shoot and not say anything?" Her voice was almost pleading.

The Boss's demeanor changed. His jaw tightened and he seethed, "I gave a warning shot and said, *Hold it!*"

Sandra remained as composed as she could. She'd learned that showing fear had seldom been to her advantage. "No you didn't! I heard a gun, and then Stew yelled, '*I'm shot! They shot me!*'"

"Well, I had to shoot a couple of them because it's easier to take them in that way."

"But why did you shoot Mike? His hands were in the air!"

"Because he smarted off to me! That don't work. I lost my temper and shot him!" the Boss sputtered. Sandra could feel his anger swelling, and she worried she had pushed him too far. He'd become agitated so she switched gears.

"Who else did you think was a girl?" She tried to turn the tables, make it sound like she was questioning him without sounding accusatory.

"That long-haired fourteen-year-old. That *hippie.*"

"He is not! He's a sweet kid. His hair is long, but it's always clean and never dirty like some guys with long hair."

"When I say hippie, I just use that as a word to call them or describe them. There's really not any hippies around here like in California and those places." He seemed to be grasping at explanations, and Sandra let his words sink in while planning her strategy. The engine hummed, and Sandra noticed an occasional clunking sound. The radio was off, the dash was dirty, and papers and cans were strewn about the floorboard. It wasn't how she pictured an official police vehicle. The Boss was tense and talking seemed to calm him. His scattered conversation broke her concentration.

"You know, all night tonight your friends will be blowing up balloons every hour on the hour. Then the police can tell just how much grass they've been smoking." He kept glancing in his rearview mirror. "I wonder where my buddies are. Every time there's a drug raid, they drive around in the cars while I have the truck." She wasn't sure what he even meant by that. "Just in case the sheriff insists on seeing you, you need to drink this Coke," he said, handing her a can of soda. "Drink it, and they won't be able to tell you've been smoking. There's a certain acid in this Coke that kills the scent of the grass. Then they can't bust you."

Sandra agreed to drink it even though she'd never heard of such a thing. Her gut instinct told her things didn't add up. It was all so strange. Yet she had no choice but to go along with him. She was also desperate to avoid getting busted. She wanted to believe him. They drove down back roads, some paved, some gravel, turning here and there. Sometimes the Boss was silent for long stretches. Always his head was bobbing back and forth, and every so often he'd crane his neck toward the windshield as if looking for a certain landmark or road up ahead.

Suddenly he let out a deep sigh and tapped his forehead with the palm of his hand. "I remember! I was supposed to meet my buddies back at the next drug raid." He pulled a wide U-turn on the road, and in no time they were headed back from where they'd come. He continued driving, and Sandra began to wonder how many dark country roads surrounded by endless fields they would have to traverse. Finally, she could no longer stand the nerve-racking quiet.

"Where are we going?"

"An abandoned house where we think drugs are stored," he answered quickly, which surprised her. "We have to raid one more place tonight."

They continued, making occasional turns until he finally slowed and turned into a long drive leading to what appeared to be an abandoned house with sagging windows and the dilapidated remains of a former barn. A rusty barbed-wire fence that leaned nearly to the ground in places surrounded the house. The soft glow of headlights from a car already in the farm yard slashed through the still night.

"They are already here," the Boss said.

Sandra's heart jumped. She hoped that when the Boss said "they" he meant his partners and the boys. *Maybe the cops decided to bring the boys with them.* She hoped to see Roger in the backseat and sat up expectantly, tilting her head at just the right angle to avoid the glare of the window, striving to get a glimpse of his face. Instead, the car door opened to reveal the stern silhouettes of J.R. and Hatchet Face. The Boss jumped out of the pickup, gave Sandra

75

a don't-you-dare look, and left the door partially open while the three men stood halfway between the two vehicles. Sandra saw J.R. and Hatchet Face exchange puzzled looks when they saw her, and she thought they seemed very surprised that she was here at the drug raid. *Maybe they thought I'd be with the sheriff or something.*

Hatchet Face spoke first. "We needed to take care of some other business. We told the sheriff she was just drunk," he said, nodding toward Sandra. "But he still wants to see her, so keep her with you. I'll talk to him on the radio later and get it all straightened out because she's kind of dumb and scared right now."

The Boss seemed edgy. "What did you guys do back at the park after I left?"

"Ha! All four of them tried to get away," J.R. laughed.

"Did they say anything? Ask about the girl?"

"Yeah, that Roger asked where she was." His voice dropped on the last word as if to indicate it was a stupid question.

Sandra perked up at the mention of Roger's name. A damp gleam of hope sprang into her eyes.

"How are the four boys?" she asked.

J.R. sneered. He glared at Sandra; his fixed stare bored right through her. Creepy and deviant, his appearance alarmed Sandra. There was an ugly feel to him.

"When he came to, they all tried to get away," he finally answered coldly.

"Roger came to from the tranquilizer gun?" she asked quietly. He wasn't as easy to talk to as the Boss. There was something unsettling about him, like a curled snake that could strike at any moment.

The man nodded. In spite of the horrors of the last hours, her hopes soared at the thought of Roger waking groggy but safe from the tranquilizer.

The Boss seemed to have more questions, but J.R. brushed him off. He had his own agenda.

"I'll stay here and make sure she don't go nowhere," he told the Boss and Hatchet Face.

To Sandra's dismay, once the two men stepped away from the vehicle, J.R. came over to the pickup, his thick figure filling the open doorway. He climbed in next to her. His mouth was curled into a lewd half-smile, and his eyes looked ravenous.

Chapter 21

J.R.'s awkward hands descended on her body almost immediately. "Take your pants off!" he ordered through gritted teeth. His foul breath was an assault on Sandra's nostrils and she automatically twisted away from his revolting bulk. "Your underpants too!"

Sandra froze. Her mind couldn't process these words as his coarse hands groped at her body. His evil voice and harsh touch made her feel that fighting back was useless. Trembling, she began unsnapping her jeans and felt bile rising from her stomach. J.R. felt she was moving too slowly, so he shoved her hands away and yanked her pants off. He threw himself on her like a beast, and a sharp pain pierced her body. His labored breathing was hot against her neck, and he swung his forearm aggressively, knocking her head against the door of the pickup in the process. J.R. grabbed a handful of her hair and pulled her head up, staring into her panicked eyes.

The pain continued, the violence escalated. From somewhere deep within, a survival instinct kicked in, mentally removing her from the situation, and she immediately felt a sense of detachment. It was as if she were floating and looking down on her body. Her mind was reaching to make sense of what was happening. *The girls at school are not going to believe this when I tell them what happened!* The thoughts didn't match what was happening to her body, but then it seemed as if only a moment had passed and just as quickly, the loathsome man was lifting himself off of her. She heard the door slam behind him and found herself alone in the silent, dark cab of the pickup. The open door had let in a stream of cool, fresh air yet his repugnant scent still lingered at the tips of her nostrils.

Demoralized, Sandra sluggishly pulled her underwear and pants back on, crossed her arms over her stomach, then with one hand reached up subconsciously and pulled her long hair to the front, stroking it over and over and pulling lightly to smooth out the tangles that had formed moments ago. She felt defiled. The man was just outside the door leaning with his back against the truck and waiting for his partners' return. A white-hot flash of terror spread from the pit of her stomach through her trembling body. She thought she might vomit but choked back the urge. It gave her a small feeling of control. Sandra's experiences at the hands of a cruel foster family and heavy-handed nuns had taught her that adults in charge often abused their power. In her traumatized mind, she still wanted to believe that he was a cop. This was what she had to live through to get out of the charges and avoid spending the rest of her teenage years in a detention center.

When the Boss and Hatchet Face emerged from the darkness a short time later, the three men stood near the pickup. A strange energy had developed among them now, and they all seemed to be talking at once then occasionally breaking into uncontrollable laughter. *They're talking crazy*, Sandra thought. Their conversation jumped from one idea to the next, and every other sentence was punctuated with a wild whoop or laugh. It sounded as if they didn't know where to go next. Stay here. No, go to the lake. Go to the farm. Nearly an hour had passed since they'd arrived at the abandoned house, and their words pounded in her ears. Sandra closed her eyes and took deep breaths to stave off the shaking. It was hard to think straight.

The three killers walked toward the abandoned house and stood in a circle, speaking in hushed voices out of earshot of Sandra.

"You screwed up!" Hatchet Face directed his words at the Boss.

"I didn't have time! I—"

"I'll do it," J.R. offered in a steady voice.

"Shut up! I'll take care of the girl. I have a club, or I have my shotgun." The Boss already had blood on his hands tonight. He was ready to take down another innocent victim to eliminate any witnesses.

"Let's take care of her right here," Hatchet Face countered.

The Boss ignored him. "I'll take care of the girl. We'll meet back at the farm."

They returned to the pickup where Sandra had been left waiting. "Look," Hatchet Face told her, "I talked to the sheriff on the radio, and he was bragging about making this next drug raid himself and taking all the people alone so he gets all the credit. That ain't gonna happen." He turned to J.R. "I'm going to find the sheriff. You coming with me?" The two men got in the car and drove off, leaving Sandra and the Boss in the blackened farm yard with only a dome light illuminating the face of the psychotic killer and the girl who'd lost her innocence a short time ago.

Hatchet Face gave J.R. a shove on the arm and howled uncontrollably before gaining composure. "I better get you back to your second home before you get us all in trouble. You were supposed to be back a looonnng time ago."

"Don't forget your *job* either. Don't screw up like the Boss did back at the farm. With that... girl," J.R. said.

The car sped toward downtown Sioux Falls until it came to a stop in front of a large brick building. It was the Minnehaha County Jail, J.R.'s second home. He'd been incarcerated in the county jail on various convictions. The jail had a work release program where, if granted permission by the administration, an inmate was allowed to sign out and return to lock-up following a work shift. J.R. had obtained a job at a towing company which allowed him the liberty to work flexible hours since the tow trucks operated around the clock. He had checked out of jail at 6:30 AM on November seventeenth and clocked out of his job at 3:00 PM. He didn't check back into jail until 2:30 AM on November eighteenth. When word of this eventually came to light, enraged citizens demanded an explanation, and the entire work release system was revamped.

After dropping off J.R., Hatchet Face drove to a large slough, known as Grass Lake, northwest of Sioux Falls. The two men had concluded on the drive into town that they needed to ditch their weapons. Hatchet Face had stolen his shotgun anyway, so easy come easy go. He grabbed the two shotguns from the trunk and walked to the water's edge. He grasped the barrel of one shotgun and heaved it, watching it flip end over end before making a loud splash and disappearing beneath the murky water. The second shotgun soon followed, and Hatchet Face wiped his hands on the sides of his jeans before heading back to the car with a satisfied smile on his face. He was certain J.R. would be pleased with this, although not much ever seemed to please J.R. He hadn't slipped up like the Boss, who'd failed to get rid of that girl back at the farm. They'd given the Boss a second chance though, when he'd told them that he was thinking of using the club on her. *She's probably dead by now,* he thought briefly before a disturbing realization crossed his mind. Deer hunting season was around the corner, and now neither of them had a slug gun.

Inside the cab of the truck, Sandra felt as if her insides had stopped. Just completely stopped. Her breathing, her heart, even her blood felt as if it had just stopped while her brain tried to make sense of what had happened to her body. Images of the loathsome J.R., his revolting breath, and awkward hands on her body flooded through her mind. Sandra gulped quick, shallow breaths and tried to regain her composure.

"What's going on?" she asked the Boss, breathing out each word faintly and fearing what she thought was about to happen.

The Boss didn't respond.

"I was a virgin, you know." She shrugged, her voice deflated.

"No you weren't!" he said in a wary voice.

"I'm only thirteen."

The Boss stared silently with his brow wrinkled in deep concentration. He seemed unmoved, but her words had affected him in a way that changed the course of the night. "I'm gonna see how much guts you have," he finally said.

She felt as if her mind had been trapped in a wheel spinning around and around but going nowhere yet Sandra forced herself to get out of the vehicle at his command. She thought she knew what was going to happen next, but her mind wouldn't accept it. Every action was blending together, and nothing was making sense. Next to her, the Boss began shoving away used cups and papers from under the passenger's seat and soon pulled out a large, broken ax handle that he'd occasionally used as a club on pesky farm dogs that wouldn't leave him alone. He then reached in the glove box and removed a flashlight, which he handed to Sandra.

"I'm gonna take you in that old house and try to scare you to death...BOO! BOO!" Then he began laughing raucously with wheezy rasps before turning strangely quiet. "Get going!" He ordered her over to one of the broken out windows. She stood her ground, refusing to move until he shoved her and turned her around by the shoulders. The Boss walked close behind, directing her to the window. "Now, look inside! You're gonna go into that room next. By yourself. And look for some critters that need to be killed."

Sandra plodded, taking note of her surroundings and evaluating her options. She peered in the window, sweeping the flashlight from side to side. Dead branches and what looked like wadded up and decaying curtains littered the warped floor. A claw-like scritching sound scuttered across the debris, causing her to jump back. It was all so abnormal. "This is weird. I'm not going in there." She kept her voice even and looked at the Boss.

He stared her down before shaking his head in disgust. "Get back in the pickup." His voice was flat or weary, Sandra wasn't sure, and it was the continual uncertainty of the night that had beaten her down. She sneaked a glance at his watch in the brief moments that the dome light was on. It was 4:30 AM. She was exhausted, terrified, and on the brink of collapsing. Against the rhythmic thumping of the tires on blacktop, she fought to stay awake.

On several occasions that night, Sandra had lost track of time, and under the shroud of sleeplessness the events of the night had melded into a haze. Whenever she glanced at the Boss's face, his eyes were narrowed and his mouth set in a tight clench. It appeared to Sandra that he was unsure of his actions. Each time she'd gotten in the truck that night, things had spun further out of control.

"Where do you live?" he asked unexpectedly.

The question caught Sandra off guard, and she hesitated. If she told him where she lived he might hurt her family.

"If you don't tell me where you live, I can't take you home. And if you tell anyone what I look like or what my partners look like, we will come and get you good."

"Are you taking me home?" She allowed herself to hope. His voice sounded softer, and she found herself believing him.

"I'll take you home, but if you tell anyone what happened I'd go to prison but only for five years because I'm a cop. When I got out you'd pay for it." He shot her a determined look. "What's your phone number?"

Sandra gave it to him, afraid he'd change his mind if she refused.

"If I'm ever back this way, I'll call you and bring a little black book I keep that has all the people's names in Sioux Falls that are dealing grass or have turned people in." She didn't know what he meant.

He slowed every so often and asked Sandra which way to go to get home. When they finally turned down the road to her house, and she caught sight of the front yard, Sandra almost cried. The Boss pulled over by the mailbox at the side of the road and let her out.

Chapter 22

Sandra didn't wait for him to leave. She raced to the front door and bolted it shut behind her. The familiar scent of last night's fried hamburger with onions still hung vaguely in the air. Had that just been last night? Less than twelve hours ago? She felt as if she'd aged years since then. Sandra pulled back the curtain in the front window and saw the taillights of the pickup fading into the distance. The only sound in the room was the quiet *tick tick tick* of the clock on the wall. It was five o'clock in the morning. Everyone was asleep.

The fear-induced adrenaline surging through her veins was tempered by the overwhelming need for sleep. She crept upstairs, choosing to wake her brother rather than her mom. She was still confused and unsure of how her mom would respond. "Bob, wake up. Wake up!" she whispered, shaking his shoulder until he was fully awake. As she rolled out the story, it was hard for her to believe the words coming from her own mouth.

"You've got to call the police because they don't sound like real cops."

"But what if they are and I turn them in?"

"Well, you've got to do something!"

"They know where I live! I gave them our phone number."

"Go get some sleep and think about it."

Sandra went to her room, propped her pillow against the headboard, and leaned against it, hugging the pillow tightly and letting its familiar scent fill her nostrils. She saw the clock change to six and then to seven. At some point, she drifted into a restless semi-sleep until she bolted awake at nine o'clock. The sun was up, and her mom was already gone.

Ring ring ring ring. Sandra tried calling Roger's house over and over, but no one answered. Then she tried Debbie. No answer again. She called another friend and finally someone picked up the phone.

Sandra didn't realize her voice had turned parched and croaky. "Can you come over? It's really important." She didn't give any more details. Her brain was foggy, and she felt nauseated. She desperately needed someone to talk with to help her make decisions. Should she try to find Roger? Should she go to the police? Were they in trouble?

"I'll come over after church."

"Can you come *now?*"

"I wish, but my mom said I *have* to go today."

Sandra hung up the phone and called Roger's house again. After dozens of tries, his mom answered.

"Is Roger home?"

"Who's calling?"

"Sandra."

"He hasn't come home all night. We don't think he did because I went upstairs this morning to put some clothes in the boys' room, and he wasn't there."

"Do you think he went somewhere? Maybe with Dana?"

"I don't think so, but I'll check and see if he's there right now."

The sound of the receiver being set on a hard surface clanked in Sandra's ear, and she could hear his mom shouting Roger's name repeatedly in the background. Then she picked up the receiver again.

"No, he's not home."

"Has anybody called?"

"No."

"If you hear anything, let me know because I'll call back later."

Roger had lived near many of his childhood friends who were so close they were more like brothers, so it wasn't unlike them to spend the night at each other's houses without even telling their parents.

A patch of sun streamed in the window, spreading its glow over a corner of the living room. Sandra sat in the warm light with her head resting on the cushiony arm of the couch, but sleep evaded her. Finally a loud knock at the door brought Sandra to her feet. It was her friend who was back from church. The story spilled out, and the friend agreed to help her any way she could. The two set out on foot for the interstate that led to Sioux Falls and on to Gitchie Manitou. Sandra wanted to return to the campsite to see if the boys were still there. Maybe if she went back out to the park, she'd find some answers to what had happened during the horrible night, her young mind rationalized. Sandra was desperate to find Roger, and with no ride the girls decided to hitchhike into Sioux Falls then out to Gitchie Manitou. They stood alongside the interstate with their thumbs out, and a lady in a beat-up car soon stopped and brought them as far as Sioux Falls, where she let them out at a phone booth on a busy street several miles from Roger's house.

Sandra called Roger's house again, praying he'd be the one to answer.

"Hello?" It was one of Roger's brothers.

"This is Sandra. Has anyone heard from Roger yet?"

She kept desperately talking without even pausing to listen.

"I know what happened to him because I was with him at Gitchie Manitou last night." Her mind was weary, and the words started rolling out of control. "These three guys came up and shot him and said they were cops and the bullets weren't real that it was tranquilizers." She paused for a breath.

"Sandra, slow down, I—"

"One of them raped me."

He hesitated for just a moment. There was something she needed to know, but he couldn't tell her over the phone. "Where are you? I'm coming to pick you up."

What Roger's brother hadn't told her was that his family had already received the news that Roger was dead. Instead, he remained steadfast and brought the girls to the police station, where a detective wearing a dark suit directed Sandra and Roger's brother into a cramped office.

"This is the girl who was with my brother," he explained to the detective.

87

The detective's steeled eyes exuded seriousness. He got right to the point. "There has been a homicide," he said, looking at Sandra. "Do you know what a homicide is?" The way he asked the question indicated she should know. Sandra didn't want to appear stupid so she answered yes even though she didn't know. Her life experiences to this point could be wrapped up in what she'd learned from TV shows like *The Brady Bunch* and *Mutual of Omaha's Wild Kingdom*. Upon hearing that, the man closed the door behind them and immediately began reading Sandra her rights.

The moment he heard this, Roger's brother flew into a rage. "What the *&%$ is this? This girl was with those boys. She's a victim, too!" With his long hair and strong voice, he reminded Sandra of an older version of Roger but never so much as now when he jumped to her defense, a girl he barely knew.

Sandra's mind was straying into a strange zone of being wide awake yet yearning for sleep to wash away the horrid memories of the previous night. Her greatest comfort at the moment was that Roger's brother had taken charge and defended her.

"Sir, this is standard police procedure, and I need to ask you to leave the room." The detective's sober face did nothing to ease the sick gnawing in Sandra's stomach. After repeated attempts at persuading the detective to let him stay, Roger's brother was eventually led out of the room, still protesting Sandra's treatment.

Soon another policeman entered and herded Sandra down the hall for mug shots and then fingerprinting. Sandra bristled but she was light-headed from lack of sleep and nauseated from lack of food. After washing the dark-staining ink from her fingers, he guided her into a small bare room with a single table, fluorescent overhead lights, and an assortment of mildly comfortable chairs. It would have been a quietly nondescript place had it not been for the task before her. The investigators now needed her handwritten account of everything she could remember from the night of horrors.

"Include everything you can remember: colors, sounds, names. Sometimes it's the small things that help us solve a case," she was instructed. And write she did. The investigator sat by, silently composing his own report. By the time she was finished, a ten-page account lay fanned out on the table before them. He was impressed by her determination yet something was amiss. The problem was that her story just didn't add up. There was no apparent motive according to her version, and the likelihood was pretty slim that three men would just appear out of nowhere and murder four strangers for no reason. Then there was the fact that she had not been murdered. To top it off, the detectives seemed to have the same gnawing question: why would a murderer drop her off at her house? The whole situation was highly suspicious. There had to be something she wasn't telling them.

How was it that this girl, who had witnessed the murder of her boyfriend, could garner enough composure to write so determinedly without once breaking down? Wouldn't the natural reaction to hearing about her boyfriend's death be to break down and cry? He'd been stunned when she'd simply nodded silently at being told of the homicides. And now, here she sat, scribbling away without a hint of emotion, not a smile, not even a grimace. She was like a machine that didn't stop. One word kept coming to his mind: cold.

The reality was that Sandra didn't know what the word "homicide" meant. She had pieced enough information together to establish that it had to mean there had been a crime and perhaps it had something to do with drug raids. She had been informed that the three men from the previous night were not cops, and she was determined to use every last bit of strength to catch these criminals. Sandra pushed herself past her limit. She was so drained it took all her strength and concentration just to keep her eyes open. She found that if she wrote without stopping, her body resisted shutting down. When she paused, exhaustion overcame her, which is why she hadn't stopped writing until the final detail left her pen. It was up to her to provide the information to catch these offenders.

By the time Sandra completed her handwritten report, a captain and lieutenant from the detective bureau had been assembled with two quick phone calls. They took over the investigation and began questioning Sandra about the previous night. Both read the detective's initial report, their eyes settling on the word "cold." They added the information to their folders, yet were prepared to explore all possibilities about the girl at this point as they'd been trained. The sheet of questions they held were carefully designed to not only glean information but would be used to eventually try to winnow out inconsistencies in her answers. First, though, they would just let her talk. Sandra didn't know it at the time, but there had already been discussions throughout the police department that the girl who'd shown up as an unexpected witness probably had more to do with the case than she'd be willing to admit.

A dull pounding, exacerbated by fatigue, pulsed from the top of her head down to her neck. The two detectives, one much younger than the other, shuffled through important-looking folders, and one of them looked up at Sandra with suspicion. Another man entered the room; he introduced himself to her as Sheriff Craig Vinson, then leaned over and whispered something to a woman sitting at the table ready to take shorthand notes. They both glanced over at Sandra. Vinson introduced the woman to Sandra as the person who would record a written account of the interview. The woman nodded politely and returned to the notes on her clipboard. Sandra reeled at having been read her rights, and her guilt seemed to be the overwhelming consensus. She'd seen the suspicious looks and heard the accusatory tones. Yet, for the first time since arriving at the station, she felt a wisp of trust, and it hovered in the air between Sandra and Vinson. She'd immediately warmed to his soothing voice and good manners. Qualities that reminded her of Roger.

The three men pulled their chairs up around the table, and one of them turned on a tape recorder. It whirred to life. Sandra took a deep breath, ready to give her statement.

Chapter 23

The first questions were easy: What is your date of birth? Where do you go to school? How many brothers and sisters do you have? Then came the part she dreaded.

"Tell us everything that happened last night starting with the phone call from Roger."

Sandra found herself reliving the nightmare with each lengthy explanation. Never once stopping and asking for a break, she answered with details that painted a night of horror and refused to quit until she'd unloaded every strange memory that had been gnawing away at her weary mind.

"Honey, you've been through a lot." Vinson's jowly voice was calming. "You rest now. I've got your mother on the way."

Sandra gratefully laid her head onto her folded arms, not even aware she'd dozed until her mother's soft touch startled her awake. Lolo grabbed her daughter in a tight embrace and stroked her hair that was now matted with the grime of dirt paths and lost innocence.

"Ma'am, your daughter provided excellent information. We hope it will prove very useful in catching the murderers," Vinson said reassuringly.

Sandra looked into her mother's eyes and whispered, "Murderers?"

Is that what homicide meant? Breathless, she sat wondering if it could really be true. *Were Roger and the other boys really dead? How could this be happening?*

But moments later, reality set in and Sandra collapsed onto the floor and broke into fitful, choking sobs. Lolo enveloped her daughter with loving arms and tried to absorb her pain, but it was no use. For Sandra, her anguish had reached its climax and exploded, sending her into hysterics.

As Lolo and Vinson discussed the agenda for the investigation, Sandra clung to her mother, shuddering. She wasn't sure what they were talking about because even though she heard their words, the meaning just bounced off her brain. Somehow they managed to transport her into a car, and then she was vaguely aware of being ushered into a sterile white room with an unsettling bright light overhead. Lolo was immediately removed from Sandra's side and a stream of strangers, men in white medical coats, filed into the room, making notes on their clipboards and spewing out more words she didn't understand about pelvic examinations and speculums. Although she was now clothed in a thin gown, it felt as if her body was being violated again, this time by the group of men wearing medical masks . She held her breath and tried to block out what was happening "down there" by thinking of words to her favorite song, praying to God for this to end, and counting down the seconds until she could run to Lolo's arms again. Then, as if a biting wind had finally passed through, the men were suddenly not there anymore. The last one wordlessly left the room and shut the door with a soft click. An officer she didn't recognize drove her and Lolo back to the police station. Surely, Sandra thought, the worst was over.

While Sandra wept with a fervor brought on by a combination of lost love, trauma, and violation, the policemen in the next room determined their next move. At the top of the list was finding a safe place for Sandra and her family. Three killers were presumably at large, and they knew where she lived. The possibility had been raised that perhaps Sandra knew the killers, and this needed to be taken into consideration. A love triangle? Would she try to run? It was Sunday evening, and their choices were limited. It was ultimately decided that she would spend the night at the juvenile detention center for her own safety, as it was put. Tomorrow, the department would find a safe house for the whole family.

That night, on a thin, institutional-grade mattress, Sandra eventually fell into a restless sleep only to awake screaming. All alone, she was once again separated from the person who held the power to comfort her. Lolo, who was staying at the home of a friend along with the rest of the family, longed to take away her beautiful daughter's pain and yearned for time to heal her. Neither could have known that the worst was not over. There was taxing work ahead for Sandra. Although exhausted, she made the commitment to compose herself for the sake of the boys who were now, as she'd been reminded several times that night, in a better place.

The house was dark and still when Vinson arrived home many hours later. He turned on a small lamp and saw someone had left him a note on the table.

Terrible game! You didn't miss much. Bears scored in the first quarter, and then it was a washout. Bears: 7, Lions: 30

Had that been just this afternoon? Any importance he'd attached to the game had vanished in the wake of the day's events. Vinson didn't feel like the same man who'd left the house expecting to find himself on the receiving end of a prank.

He crept down the hallway and shut the bathroom door before turning on the light to avoid waking anyone. In the mirror, he saw a man who should have been in bed hours ago, but those who knew him would have see a man filled with the determination that would eventually be the key to cracking the case. He'd started this assignment, and he'd see it out to the end. He'd even brought with him some files to look over before going to bed. There were some names he might need to check out the next day. They still had few clues, and Vinson was well aware that the success of the entire case could likely fall on the shoulders of a thirteen-year-old girl. This small-town sheriff had been thrust into the eye of the storm, and there were some who wondered if he possessed the qualifications and experience to take the reins of such a high-profile case. In time, he and his deputy would show themselves as capable as any in rising to the occasion.

Chapter 24
November 19, 1973

On Monday morning, Sandra should have been getting ready for school, blow-drying her hair to a shine, eating a Pop-Tart, then giggling through the school hallways with friends. Instead, she was escorted back to the police station by Vinson for a meeting with a woman who would develop a composite sketch of each perpetrator based on Sandra's descriptions.

The sketch artist immediately put Sandra at ease, asking which movies she'd seen and discovering that they shared a fondness for *The Brady Bunch*. Sandra was also relieved that the lady didn't require her to relive the horrors she endured. "Just tell me everything you can remember about what each man looked like." The work was more grueling than Sandra had anticipated. The lady pulled out some reference photos; each one had a slightly different nose or mouth, whichever feature Sandra was describing. Each trait she described brought back a spark of terror. She pored through the pictures until she found the feature that most closely resembled the monster she was describing.

"No, the face needs to be a little thinner, right there," Sandra pointed to the cheekbones of the Boss, and the sketch artist patiently made the adjustment, "and his hair was shorter on the sides and kind of spiky or wavy on top." The only noise was the humming of overhead lights and the scratching sound of the pencil moving quickly across paper. After multiple adjustments, a hauntingly familiar face stared out from the paper. "Yes! That looks like him, that looks like the Boss," Sandra exclaimed, her stomach clenched.

After a night of erratic slumber and a morning spent staring into the hand-drawn faces of the killers, she wanted nothing more than to sleep. There was no time for that. The case could grow cold.

Sandra was loaded into a police vehicle and brought back to Gitchie Manitou. When she first heard about this plan, she nearly vomited.

"I can't do it! I don't want to see that campsite again or walk past the spot where Roger was killed! I know I can show you where everything happened on a map or something," she pleaded.

Her protests waned when the detective explained the importance of the task. Having her firsthand account filmed at the scene of the crime could eventually be the key to getting the criminals convicted in court. She had to do this. For the boys. And so she did without further complaint. The ordeal proved so traumatic that Sandra blocked the entire incident from her memory until the film was eventually brought up in court almost a year later. She was shocked to recall that she had gone back to the park so soon after the murders.

Behind the scenes, Vinson, Griesse, and the detectives worked feverishly to consolidate the information that would be released to the press. By now, the Iowa Bureau of Investigation had also been called in to assist. Vinson jotted information on a brief memo that he'd later distribute to every officer working the case. Communication was vital. So far Vinson had assessed that everyone on this case was a team player. He intended to keep it that way by being forthcoming with information, delegating responsibility, and remaining neutral about the case's only witness.

The latter choice would be the one divisive issue among the group. Nonetheless, Vinson and another detective had already mapped out possible locations for the farm and the abandoned house where the rape had occurred. The massive "hot zone," as they referred to it, covered hundreds of miles of roads. Along with Sandra, they would drive along a predetermined course, working their way from the edge of Sioux Falls outward. Sandra had affirmed that she would definitely remember both places if she saw them again. A search of this zone could conceivably take weeks, yet it was one of the only leads they had to follow. Some of his fellow officers tried to dissuade him from pulling man hours away from the investigation to focus on a farm and abandoned house that they didn't believe existed. Later that day, however, Vinson and another detective began the search by car along with Sandra's help.

First, though, there was the issue of covertly transferring Sandra and her family to a safe house, where they would stay until the murderers were apprehended. The safe house was a small trailer that sat on a sparsely populated street in Sioux Falls. The house was furnished with only the bare necessities, and this is where the family stayed while the hunt for three ruthless killers went on around them. Unmarked police cars performed regular security checks of the trailer. Yet, there was mounting concern down at the police station that Sandra was withholding information.

There were divided opinions on Sandra's credibility. Many officers had expressed concern either directly to Vinson or among each other in private conversations that Sandra knew the men, or at least one of the men who committed the murders. It seemed unlikely that everyone except her would have been murdered. And why had only one of the men raped her? The common consensus was that it was a scorned boyfriend. Otherwise, why would he let her go and drop her off at home? But Vinson and several others had a gut feeling about Sandra's innocence. Either way, there was mounting pressure to find the killers, who were still at large. Already there was an outcry from the community to lock up these three supposed murderers running loose and dangerous.

While the detectives meticulously followed up on their limited clues, Sandra had another concern on her mind. She wanted to see the boys at the funeral home. Whenever the officer assigned to the safe house stopped in, she used her fiercest arguments, even breaking down into tears, to persuade him into letting her see the boys.

"I understand what you're asking. But you have to know that our top priority is keeping you safe," he explained sympathetically.

"I WILL be safe. You'll be there, right?" she countered.

"It's more complicated than that. There are too many people milling around the funeral home. If the killers are determined to eliminate you as a witness, that would be a prime opportunity for them. They could even be staking out the funeral home in hopes of following you back here."

In the end, it was one argument that Sandra lost.

In spite of not being allowed a visit to the funeral home, Sandra was unrelenting in her requests to attend Roger's funeral. She hounded her mother, then the officers assigned to the safe house, and finally to Sheriff Vinson. "If you don't let me go, I'll walk there by myself," she said, determined to see Roger one last time.

The officers and Vinson tried to remain steadfast. There were three killers at large who were likely focused on disposing of the only remaining eyewitness. The public was already clamoring for arrests to be made, so they couldn't chance losing another child. Sandra was persuasive, and in the end, Vinson couldn't ignore her heartfelt pleas. He made arrangements that he thought were suitable to everyone. She would be allowed to attend the funeral but would sit in a small overflow room adjacent to the chapel. A heavy curtain that divided the two rooms would be shut, and a plainclothes officer would be nearby. As soon as the funeral was over, she'd have to leave. The detectives had a meeting to troubleshoot any potential problems that could occur. Everyone agreed that the plan seemed safe. So Vinson finalized all the details. All the details he could predict at that time.

Chapter 25
November 19, 1973

As medical examiners, Dr. Gessford and Dr. Schultz had performed their share of autopsies due to unusual causes of death. Yet conducting the autopsies of four grisly murders remained a difficult task. Their work involved setting aside emotions in order to collect facts, and both were experts at this methodical process. Even with extensive experience and training, Gessford and Schultz had to steel themselves for the examination of four teenage boys who'd been gunned down in their youth.

The day was emotionally exhausting, and at the end they reviewed the four separate reports they'd prepared. The doctors anticipated eventually being summoned to court and called on to explain and defend these reports in a challenging cross-examination. Both proceeded carefully, as always, double checking each notation.

Roger Essem, male, 17 years old. Multiple wounds to the head, face, upper chest, and arms. Seven exit wounds. Skull fractures. Brain wounds.

Stewart Baade, male, 18 years old. Wounds to the chest, abdomen, and right upper leg. Extensive wounds to the left hand. Large, gaping wound to middle of back and buttocks.

Mike Hadrath, male, 15 years old. Wounds to the upper left chest, left upper arm, left side of face, left hand, and wrist. Also shots to the back, buttocks, and legs. One of the pathologists reviewed the notes where he determined this had happened after the initial wounds and while the victim was likely lying face down on the ground.

Dana Baade, male, 14 years old. Wounds to the right chest, heart, and back.

The pathologists also removed what was later determined by ballistics experts to be #4 and double-ought buckshot from the bodies of Stew and Mike, #4 buckshot from Roger, and double-ought buckshot from Dana.

Chapter 26

Sandra thought that attending the funeral would provide some relief, some sense of closure. Instead, the pain intensified. A strangely unsettling woe tore at her insides. She'd never been a worrier; however, she both dreaded and yearned for the time of the funeral to arrive knowing it would be the last time she'd see Roger.

She rummaged through the clothes her mom had hastily packed. Fortunately there was an adequate amount of black clothing to choose from, and Sandra tugged and fussed with the fabric of her outfit in front of a cloudy mirror pocked with dark spots. She tried to put her hair up in an elegant bun, but she'd never worn her hair that way and the result was disastrous. She brushed her hair out again, choosing to wear it straight, the only way Roger had ever seen her.

An officer arrived at the safe house in an unmarked car with dark windows and instructed her to sit in the back. Arriving to the funeral at the same time as the other mourners, he drove around to an inconspicuous entrance. She'd barely exited the vehicle, when the side door opened, and she was hurried into a small, empty room with the curtain closed for her own protection. She wrinkled her nose at the sickly-sweet smell of funeral flowers.

Roger and the other boys had been popular. The funeral was packed to capacity with standing room only and mourners lined up out the door. Sandra couldn't see anyone but could hear muffled conversations in hushed voices and occasional loud sobs. She stared into her lap and imagined people on the other side politely taking turns gazing mournfully at Roger before commenting to whoever was next to them about the beautiful flowers, then finding empty pews where they could dab at their eyes with wadded up tissues. Feeling as though she couldn't bear the sadness or pain another minute, she ached for the service to start. Loneliness descended on her, and she forced herself to momentarily silence her trembling sobs. *I can't take this anymore!* She wanted to feel the warmth of comforting arms, but bore the sorrow alone.

Sandra was unaware that not all the conversations were muffled. Beyond the decorum of the chapel, a relative of one of the slain boys loudly expressed disapproval of Sandra's presence at the funeral. This person had the same misgivings as many in the police department that Sandra was lying about what had happened that ghastly night at Gitchie. Why would a cold-blooded killer drive her home and drop her off? Who was the real killer? Perhaps a jealous boyfriend?

The distraught relative caught word that Sandra was behind the curtain, and with emotions running high, went to find her. "You get the hell out of here! You know more than you're telling the cops! I want her out of here!" the heart-broken relative screamed.

With her cover blown, Sandra had no choice but to leave Roger's funeral without ever saying her final goodbye. *It can't get any worse!* she thought. But it did.

For days details of the Gitchie murders topped headlines across the Midwest. Actual headlines read:

NO MOTIVE FOUND FOR 4 SLAYINGS;
DESCRIPTIONS OF SUSPECTS RELEASED

FOUR AREA TEENS FOUND SLAIN IN PARK

This was followed by a description detailing the limited information the police had to share with the public. There wasn't much to go on. Vinson had neither suspects nor any conclusive physical evidence that provided a trail to the murderers. The focus was on the three sketches, which would turn out to be remarkably accurate portrayals. Also, the police were asking for information about a Chevy fleet-side pickup, red and white in color with a white, wooden stock rack in the box, and a gun rack in the rear window. The windshield was cracked from left to the right center. As much as Sandra wanted to forget the horrible events that had occurred within, she had astonishingly remembered minute details, including the color of the inspection sticker in the lower corner of the windshield. And then there was the gas tank, standard farm equipment, but this one was red. In the tri-state area, an all-points bulletin was put out to law enforcement agencies. The artist's renderings of the three murderers hit the newspapers, and this set the public on edge. Yet, after several days of grueling work, hardly a clue or lead had surfaced. Doubts about Sandra's story mushroomed. She wasn't allowed to return to school or leave the safe house unattended, and accusatory whispers spread among her classmates.

The scant information available indicated that the investigation should focus on Sandra. Homicides of this nature by strangers are rare in themselves, but in the small towns surrounding Gitchie Manitou where doors often remained unlocked even at night, the thought was preposterous. One detective returned from a long day of finding nothing but false leads and sat Sandra down. His bloodshot eyes revealed the strain of the investigation.

"Enough of this! You need to tell us what you really know." His livid voice cut Sandra, adding to her feelings of helplessness. She'd told them everything she knew and had pushed herself to conjure up the horrible memories again and again and again, hoping to recall something to help the investigation. She'd endured pain beyond description, been removed from her home, her friends, her classmates, and now was being accused of covering up a violent crime. Her spirit was crushed. She wanted to stay in bed all day, still and silent with the covers pulled tight above her head to block out the light. A glimmer of hope came from knowing that Vinson believed in her.

The seasoned Lyon County Sheriff had a gut instinct that the girl was telling the truth about the unbelievable tale. He had built a reputation as a stern, headstrong sheriff who wasn't afraid to demand or go against the grain in order to get the job done. He knew that being in charge sometimes involved making decisions or having opinions that wouldn't make everyone happy. He had his focus, though, and was prepared to do everything in his power to solve this case. Every morning he and a detective picked Sandra up at the safe house and together they systematically wove their way down seemingly endless roads based on the map Vinson kept at his side. Each day more gravel, more tar roads to traverse. Since it had been dark and foggy the night of the murders and Sandra had never been to the area before, Vinson and another detective had developed a map that covered an immense area of potential locations for the farm and abandoned house.

Vinson refused to give up searching for the farm with a red gas tank. While they searched, he tried to keep Sandra's spirits up by asking about her favorite foods, family, and fun memories while growing up. The conversations were a welcome diversion from the strain of the burden she was carrying and helped forge a bond between Sandra and the sheriff. For her own protection, she was not allowed to return to school or leave the safe house unless on official police business until the killers were in custody. So daily drives along miles of remote roads, past the dried remains of last summer's cornfields and countless two-story white farm houses, gave Sandra a sense of purpose. She preferred it to sitting idly at the safe house with nothing to think about apart from the horrible night. What Vinson didn't know was that this methodical search was laying the groundwork to unravel a bizarre tale of murder straight out of a horror movie.

On this day a detective from Sioux Falls rode with them as he occasionally did. Vinson was a careful observer of his surroundings, a necessary quality for anyone conducting an investigation and part of what made him a successful sheriff. He was also blessed with the ability to bestow deep compassion or to remain professionally detached, depending on the situation. His interactions with Sandra required the former. "Are you getting tired? Do you need to rest your eyes?" She shook her head no.

As they approached another farm, Vinson slowed the car and looked over at Sandra to get a read of her face. Her hopes soared every time a glimpse of an abandoned structure or a two-story white house came into view. She couldn't believe how many of them dotted the countryside and had lost count days ago. She continued staring out the side window and shook her head. She slumped back in her seat and sighed. Giving up had never crossed her mind. The boys deserved her help, and she was the only eyewitness. It was up to her to identify the places the Boss had taken her that night. She was so unfamiliar with the area that she needed to stay focused on identifying recognizable buildings. They'd covered so much territory; shouldn't they have found the place by now? After nearly two weeks of the search, hope for finding the farm was fading quickly.

"Are you sure? I can drive back by those buildings"—he pointed to a barn several yards off the road—"and maybe something will look familiar."

She shook her head again and pointed to a metal swing set and wooden playhouse between the barn and the house. "I know this isn't the place." She swung her head around to catch Vinson's expression when he wasn't expecting it. Would he look perturbed? Disappointed? She could handle either of those, but what she couldn't bear at this point would be a look of doubt etched in the creases below his eyes. To Sandra, his eyes conveyed as much as his words. She'd watched the way his eyes transformed from hopeful to defensive when they'd caught "The Look" from some of the other officers. It was a look that questioned Vinson's leadership and blatantly challenged his view of Sandra's honesty. But now, all she saw was the same strength she'd been relying on to carry her through this far. It reminded her of the way her grandfather had looked at her when she'd at first been afraid to go into the big barn. He'd comforted her by saying it was all right to sometimes be frightened. Maybe everyone didn't believe her, but Vinson did. And her family. That was all she needed, she convinced herself for the moment.

After several hours in the car together, the conversations had dwindled to an occasional comment about the condition of the road or the number of silos bordering a farm. The car was silent save for the whine of wheels on smooth blacktop. Frustration built as the day wore on. Sandra wondered how many more times she'd disappoint them by having to say, "No, that's not the place," before they gave up on her and the search. It felt as if the entire investigation lay on her shoulders, so finding the farm was vital to bring justice for Roger and the boys.

Vinson fell under enormous pressure from all sides as well. He continued frequent communication with the families of the victims and regularly assured them the department was doing all it could to pursue justice for their loved ones. Keeping the public calm and quelling their outrage at three killers still being on the loose was a daily battle on top of everything else that had to be done. And then there was the media. Just this morning he'd picked up and just as quickly tossed aside several requests for press releases about the investigation. There was nothing more he could share at this point. Even with all of this weighing on his mind, there was something that concerned him even more. Sandra. Her determination and strength right from the beginning had reassured him. To squelch increasing protests from his fellow lawmen, however, he decided to have Sandra take a polygraph test.

"The girl's telling the truth," the expert from the Iowa Bureau of Criminal Investigation said to Vinson. Two polygraph examiners had put Sandra through an intense round of questioning. Additionally the doctor concluded that Sandra had been sexually assaulted on the night of the murders.

Vinson's confidence soared; again his hunch was right. He'd thanked God that this sole witness, their shining hope for cracking the case, hadn't crumbled under the mounting obstacles she'd had to endure. She was gradually earning a reputation as a tough but quiet girl among those who believed her story. Initially, Sandra's emotional pain had been buffered by a fuzzy layer of shock that protected her mind from the grief and trauma she'd experienced. She'd operated on instinct, moving continuously from one task to the next with hardly time to sleep. Yet, after the sting of reality had crept upon her, her eyes had turned bloodshot, and her face was dulled with grief. She talked, but with a voice that had lost its fire. She answered questions but only with brief responses. This articulate girl who'd written reams of potential evidence and answered endless questions in the wake of breakdown had withered as day after day passed with nothing but disappointment. He could see that she was fading.

Vinson switched on the radio and tuned in an upbeat country song to quell the uneasy silence. Then, remembering how Sandra had raved about a new rock 'n 'roll song, he moved the dial until the static disappeared, and Mick Jagger's voice came booming through the speakers. Vinson reasoned that was about as much rock as he could handle at the moment. He pushed thoughts of a hungry press and an anxious public from his mind to concentrate on the investigation. As sheriff, he was used to juggling many responsibilities at once and others considered him adept at being able to focus on the business at hand. Today, the job of keeping Sandra focused was up to him. Over the past several days she'd enjoyed hearing stories about his family, devouring the tales about the time he spent with his friends on the golf course.

"And you eat dinner together as a family *every* night?" she'd responded when he'd told her about his family.

"Oh, not every night. Not with this job," he laughed. "But we did all the time before I became sheriff."

She asked him questions that seemed strange at first. Did someone put plates on the table or did everyone get their own? Was there a tablecloth? Until it dawned on him that perhaps she was wondering *how* a family ate dinner together. Finally she admitted that one thing she yearned for was eating together as a family. They used to when she was a very small girl back at her grandparents' farm, but now her mom worked so much that she didn't have time for family meals. Everyone fended for themselves. What touched him was that she didn't have a hint of self-pity in her voice. She was more concerned that her mom had to work such long hours and how much the two missed each other when they were apart.

He drummed the steering wheel with his fingers a few times to break the silence before speaking. "Say, did I tell you about the time I was golfing at—"

Vinson jumped when Sandra began screaming hysterically.

Chapter 27

"THAT'S HIM! THAT'S HIM! THAT'S THE BOSS!" she shouted then shot up from her seat, frantically pointing at a white pickup that had just pulled out of a driveway in front of a two-story white farmhouse. It was headed their direction on the opposite side of the road! Vinson's foot automatically went for the brake, but he immediately stepped on the gas to regain speed. He didn't want to draw attention to his actions. It surprised him that the driver of the pickup was unfazed by the sight of a patrol car.

The detective in the backseat shouted to Vinson, "Pull over! He has—"

"I saw it. I saw it," Vinson said steadily, pulling the car sharply to the side of the road near a thatch of bushes by a bend in the road. His well-trained eye hadn't missed anything. In the rear window of the pickup, he'd seen the shotgun hanging in the rack just as Sandra had described. He couldn't risk having the driver, who was in possession of a firearm, see the girl. The detective and Sandra hurried from the patrol car and positioned themselves out of view.

Vinson made a U-turn and stepped on the pedal, rapidly gaining on the white truck ahead of him. He switched on the red lights and prepared himself for a high-speed chase. To his surprise, the vehicle immediately pulled over. Vinson radioed for backup and was out of the patrol car as soon as it came to a stop. With his service revolver in hand, he ordered the driver out of the vehicle. A lanky man with short brown hair, somewhat spiky on top emerged from the pickup. Again, just as Sandra had described.

The suspect put up no resistance and with the click of handcuffs, Allen E. Fryer, age twenty-nine, found himself in the back of a squad car headed for the county jail. The farmyard that Allen Fryer, "the Boss," had just left contained the large red gas tank for which they had been searching. He was a hired hand who worked on the farm caring for machinery and livestock. Later, one farmer he'd worked for reported that Allen spent hours cradling and polishing his shotgun in his spare time.

After his arrest in the early evening, he was read his rights and taken to the Sioux Falls Police Station, where he arrived at 7:00 PM. Allen waived his rights and was interrogated for three and a half hours by two policemen. Knowing that their every action could come under close scrutiny in court, the policemen wisely provided him with frequent breaks to eat and use the restroom. He denied knowing anything about the Gitchie murders but eventually admitted he'd hunted pheasants there that day. His brothers, David L. Fryer, "Hatchet Face," and James R. Fryer, "J.R.," were also placed in custody. Both contradicted Allen's claims. The investigative team immediately focused on Allen's brothers as suspects. The detectives separated the three men, and within minutes they were all pointing their fingers at each other. Soon Allen's story changed, and he admitted being present during the shootings but claimed he hadn't fired a single shot. The policemen brought Allen back to Gitchie, where he retraced the route he took with Sandra the night of the murders.

The brothers agreed that James had met Allen and David, who'd both been recently released from the penitentiary, and gone to hunt pheasants. All of them were felons and not allowed to possess a firearm yet all of them did. When they had no success in that area, they headed to Gitchie Manitou to poach a deer. After that, their assorted stories disintegrated, with each implicating the other in the shootings of the four boys. Soon, Allen, David, and James were facing numerous charges.

David and Allen were placed in a small jail in Rock Rapids, Iowa. James remained in the Minnehaha County jail in Sioux Falls. After almost two weeks of searching for the heinous murderers, it was a satisfying victory for Sandra. Although she still struggled to sleep and had to force herself into bed at night knowing the nightmares were waiting for her mind to slip into slumber, she knew the three brothers couldn't touch her now. She could return home. All of the questionable looks and guilty stares would now stop. She had helped put them behind bars. But for Sandra, the victory turned bittersweet. David eventually pled guilty before the trials started and was sent to Fort Madison Prison in Iowa. At about the same time, James was transferred to the Rock Rapids jail with his brother, Allen. Had Sandra known the next move James and Allen planned, she wouldn't have felt safe at all.

TOP (from left): James "J.R." Fryer, Allen "The Boss" Fryer, David "Hatchet Face" Fryer.

BOTTOM: With few leads, the manhunt focused on finding the murderers based on the composite sketches developed from 13-year-old Sandra's descriptions.

TOP LEFT: Deputy LeRoy Griesse with David Fryer

TOP RIGHT: Stew's guitar as it was found at the campsite in this crime scene photo.

BOTTOM LEFT: Sheriff Craig Vinson with Allen Fryer.

Chapter 28

In 1928, Lyon County erected a much needed two-story jail in the aptly named town of Rock Rapids situated along the winding Rock River. The jail was built in the typical style for that era with the sheriff's office downstairs and jail cells on that same level as well as on the second floor. A strong cement wall, presumably criminal-proof, separated the jail from where the sheriff lived as it was common practice at the time for the sheriff to reside in close proximity to the jail. There were no security cameras available and no around the clock staff, so Sheriff Vinson lived on-site along with his family. His wife served as the jail matron and cooked the meals for the inmates.

At some point new locks were installed on the cell doors, and unfortunately no one noticed that someone forgot to secure the bolts by welding them in place. No one until Allen Fryer arrived. After years of struggling in school, he'd dropped out in seventh grade at the age of sixteen. Although he had only a full-scale IQ of eighty-seven and extremely weak reading and writing skills, he showed a strength in the mechanical skills section. With nothing to do in his cell all day but devise a way to slip out of the charges he faced, Allen's criminal nature eventually led him to entertain the idea of an escape. He searched the cell and jail routines for potential weak spots when he unexpectedly came across the unsecured bolts.

If the jail employees had picked one word to describe Allen, it would have been slippery. The convict was wiry, manipulative, and loath to accept blame. He was determined to side-step charges one way or another. Upon discovering the bolts, Allen stuck his slender arm between the bars but wasn't able to bend it at the awkward angle required to reach them. A quick search of the sparsely furnished cell turned up just what he needed. The cell beds were attached to the walls with chains and a hook, giving Allen just what he needed. The hook fit snugly around the bolt. He replaced the hook back onto the chain and waited.

Later that evening, Vinson made his usual preparations before heading home. He filed some paperwork, checked on the inmates upstairs and down, turned off all the lights, and locked the front door of the jail. Then, in the corridor above, a thin arm slid from behind the bars, hook in hand. The jangling of metal on metal echoed through the darkened cells until each bolt had fallen to the floor with a thwack. *Clink, scrape, clink, scrape.* The door swung open, and he let out a rowdy victory whoop. Rushing to the lower level where his brother James was locked up, he was pleased to find the cell keys still hanging on a wall peg where he'd previously seen them. Soon both brothers were loose inside the jail. Allen performed a quick search of the lower level to find anything that might be helpful to them while on the run. Yet, he found nothing of use. Minutes later, they walked out the front door in their light green jail-issued coveralls that Vinson had purchased at the hardware store as the jail operated on a limited budget. The murderers were free again.

One sure sign of a career criminal is the ability to operate unnerved in situations that would cause most people extreme anxiety. That night, Allen and James moved boldly through the town, strutting confidently down the darkest streets and checking for a vehicle that was an easy mark. As they expected, the two found what they needed a few blocks away in front of a car dealership. It was an International pickup, which suited Allen perfectly, and it had a tank of gas as well as a set of keys in the ignition. The car belonged to a salesman who kept stacks of sales literature and forms in the pickup. The brothers shoved the papers out the door onto the car lot as they made their escape. Speeding down the nearest street, they headed west.

The next morning, Vinson's wife stood holding a breakfast tray in hand staring at the empty jail cell, a broken lock swinging from the open door. In times of crisis, Vinson didn't falter, panic, or second guess himself. He acted on instinct and experience, two qualities that allowed him to immediately size up a scenario and prioritize a plan of action. The moment the news left his wife's lips, he ran for the phone and dialed the Sioux Falls sheriff, a phone number he now knew by heart.

"Get Sandra to safety right away!"

Over the course of the day, Vinson and Deputy Griesse collected the few clues left behind by the escapees. "Well, Sheriff, at least the Fryers left the cell keys behind. We don't have to fork out money for new locks," Griesse, the jovial optimist, said with a grin, attempting to lighten the situation. Their budget was always stretched to the limit. Vinson failed to appreciate this humor. Down the street at the car dealership, the salesman had assumed someone hid his truck as a joke. When the sales literature was discovered strewn around the dealership lot, a red flag went up. That day an all-points bulletin was released to every law enforcement agency in the surrounding states.

In less than a week the truck was spotted in Wyoming after the Fryers struck a pedestrian with the stolen vehicle. Luckily the pedestrian was not seriously injured, and the two brothers were again in custody, offering little resistance while being recaptured. Allen and James were soon back in Iowa to face their murder charges.

Homicide investigations are notoriously complicated, and this case was muddied further by the brothers' conflicting statements of the events of that fatal night. It was clear to the detectives that the multiple stories they'd recounted were not adding up. Each brother had made numerous claims incriminating the others. Before David decided to plead guilty, officers drove him to the crime scene.

While walking through the park, he surprisingly confessed to about a dozen burglaries, allowing the police department to tie up these unsolved cases. However, he offered limited information about the night of the murders, saying he would never plead guilty because he'd told his mom he didn't do it, and he didn't want to disappoint her. Undeterred, the investigators continued their inspection of the campsite and surrounding area, noting each of David's vacillating answers. By the time the investigators wrapped things up, the prosecution was ready to storm the courtroom and nail the Fryer brothers. And the prosecution was armed with a trump card that the defense couldn't match, a thirteen-year-old star witness.

Chapter 29

On the first day of the trials, a detective slipped Sandra in through a side door of the courthouse to avoid the camera-wielding journalists and a sea of microphones. The media were yearning for a statement or photograph related to this high-profile case, but the police department implemented special protection to shield their young witness from the pressure of the press. Nonetheless, one enterprising photographer managed to capture a photo of her on the steps of the courthouse. For years to come, this image of a brave young girl standing alone and looking determined before facing ruthless killers would come to symbolize the essence of this trial. Vinson feared that a circus-like atmosphere might descend upon the trials, but the media showed restraint in their treatment of Sandra. Still, press from most of the major newspapers in the region poured into the city to write frequent reports about the proceedings.

Many courtroom spectators had been waiting anxiously for their first glimpse of the lone survivor. A hush descended and heads turned when Sandra was finally ushered in by a stone-faced bailiff. The prosecution unrolled a detailed time line of events complete with evidence, crime-scene photographs, forensics reports, testimony from ballistics experts, and every contradictory interview with the Fryer brothers. When the trial for Allen began and Sandra was finally called to the witness stand, she had to force herself to look at him. His eyes were more sinister than she'd remembered, and then there was this aura of superiority about him from his smug expression to his arrogant body language. Although her lawyer had coached her ahead of time, no one could have prepared her for how difficult the questioning would be. She'd been instructed to answer only yes or no when possible and to leave the rest of the answer open. Sandra's mom came to court with her loyally every day.

Under the glare of Allen's hate-filled stare, Sandra could hardly keep up with the defense attorney's questioning.

Attorney: And could you tell who fired the second shot?

Sandra: Allen.

Attorney: Do you know FOR SURE that it could not have been James that fired the second shot?

Sandra: Well, Allen's gun was in the air pointing at him.

Attorney: Things were happening fast at that time, is that true?

Sandra: Yes.

Attorney: So, it was very difficult for anyone to know exactly what was happening, right?

As the cross-examination progressed, the questions became more confusing and were often worded with atypical syntax that was especially confusing to a thirteen-year-old girl. They came like rapid fire, rekindling horrifying images of that night, and Sandra recoiled inside at being interrogated over her recollection of events. The fast-paced questioning appeared to be an attempt to confuse Sandra and discredit her testimony. This wasn't the first time, however, that she'd been forced to deal with intense scrutiny. For two weeks after the murder of the four boys, she'd faced an increasingly dubious public and withstood the doubtful looks thrown at her around the police station. She'd held up under the verbal attack of the angry relative at Roger's funeral. She'd been subjected to the embarrassing medical examination and been given a polygraph test, both under bright lights by men with their untelling reactions in order to prove her truthfulness. Before that, in what seemed a lifetime away, had been the adversity she'd faced at the Indian boarding school and foster homes. These struggles had toughened her fortitude and steeled her tenacity, which now allowed her to bravely testify.

Day after day, Sandra faced the questions, the testimony, the evidence, and always the memories of that night, slicing away more of her young life. The Fryers filled the room with their presence, breathing out lies with the same air she was using to bring justice for Roger, Mike, Stew, and Dana. Sometimes her quiet voice broke during testimony, but she refused to buckle under the pressure that had been building with all she'd been asked to do since the night of the murders.

The trials for the brothers lasted for more than a year, so Sandra was called upon to testify repeatedly. While the Fryers waited for their next trial date, they resided in the Lyon County Jail, which allowed Vinson and Griesse time to sum up each man's personality. Allen was wiry and cocky but had low self-esteem that he compensated for by making frequent demands he expected to be met immediately no matter how unreasonable. It was a game to him to see what he could get someone else to do for him. He had an unquenchable desire to impress others, one time claiming to Griesse that he had recently been on a hunting expedition where he'd shot wild game while leaning out the open door of an airplane. Before David had been sent to prison, he'd alternated between trying to take charge and being unsure of himself. He'd made frequent threats but rarely carried through with them. He was a follower and was also considered moody and sulky.

The one who caused the most concern was James. Words like dangerous and frightening only skimmed the surface of describing his hardened persona. He was just "off." While his brother Allen's eyes could be described as cold, James's were vacant. Unfeeling. The word that was tossed around the jailhouse was "crazy." One person associated with the trial claimed that where James's conscience should have been, there was a gaping void instead.

One afternoon, Griesse sat in the library, alert as always, on watch over James, who was taking advantage of his allotted time before returning to the courtroom. Out of nowhere, James jumped from his seat, stepped toward the officer, and bellowed, "YOU'RE NOT GONNA TAKE ME!"

The deputy leapt from his chair, knocking a stack of books to the floor, and his hand reflexively flew to his weapon. Griesse had never fired his revolver, other than in practice, and a vivid picture flashed before him of James lying dead on the floor from a gunshot wound. Though every officer understands that the call of duty may require shots to be fired, that moment when reality hits is a gut-puncher. "Don't take another step!" Griesse ordered. The rotund criminal glowered, looking ready to strike.

From the back of the room, the click of a door opening broke the heated silence, and in walked two attorneys who had arrived to prepare for trial. The two clean-shaven men with their pressed suits and leather briefcases stopped abruptly, one still holding the door open, his eyes darting between the two poised men. James sank back into his chair with a growl of disgust but never let his hostile glare leave Griesse. "You're never going to get me to Fort Madison," James announced, referring to the Iowa prison to which he'd be headed if found guilty.

The trials lingered on for months, and Sandra's role as sole witness required her to appear in court repeatedly as her testimony comprised the bulk of the evidence. The trials were popular in this area of the country where multiple murders were as rare as traffic jams. Curious murmurs bubbled through the gallery, and rubbernecking spectators clucked to each other about the shame of it all. Not only was Sandra forced to face her perpetrators day after day, but this was all played out under the curious watch of a sometimes judgmental public. During questioning she was forced to relive the nightmare in front of crowds of strangers. Sandra was a survivor, though, and she dealt with the stress, the uncomfortable questions, and the fear the only way she knew how: by pushing the ugliness to the far recesses of her mind, where they would lie dormant until one day the festering emotions would burst forth.

Eventually, the trials whose successes had depended on the guts and gumption of a young teen had finally reached their anticipated end. David had pled guilty to three counts of murder and one count of manslaughter prior to the trials. This killer who had claimed he'd never plead guilty was the first to give in. Years later in an interview with a reporter from the *Des Moines Register*,

David would claim that if "all my appeals fail, I will write the governor and ask for the death penalty. I will not live out my life in prison." He contended that living in prison is "like living with a bunch of wild hogs and other animals." He was given a life sentence without the possibility of parole.

Allen was found guilty of four counts of first degree murder. He had two prior felony convictions. In a pretrial interview, one parole officer stated that Allen had killed "in the manner of one simply poaching a deer." He was sentenced to four terms of life in prison.

James was found guilty of three counts of first degree murder and one count of manslaughter. He was given three terms of life and one term of eight years for manslaughter. The prosecution made the decision not to pursue a charge of rape since he would be locked up for life. All three were sent to the maximum security penitentiary in Fort Madison, Iowa. At the time, Iowa did not have the death penalty.

What was the motive behind the horrendous crimes at Gitchie Manitou? This was the question that so many people had pondered from the beginning. Even after lengthy court trials a clear motive was never established. Could it have been that in their twisted minds the Fryers felt they were acting as law enforcement agents and got carried away? Did they want the girl, or did James Fryer want the girl and the other brothers participated? Did Allen ask for Sandra's phone number after a night of murder because he'd developed a bizarre obsession with her? Perhaps they turned to hunting humans that night since their quest for wild game during the day had been unsuccessful, so they turned to the only prey that was available? Were they deviant psychopaths or sociopaths who refused to operate within the moral and legal boundaries of our society? The question of motive remains unanswered. One final question hung in the air: Why did Allen change his mind and decide not to kill Sandra? It was a question that would not be answered for over forty years.

TOP: The photo of Sandra that captures the emotional toll of the trials.
BOTTOM (from left): Roger Essem, Mike Hadrath, Stewart "Stew"
Baade, Dana Baade

Chapter 30

"Have I not commanded you? Be strong and courageous. Do not be frightened, and do not be dismayed for the LORD your God is with you wherever you go."

Joshua 1:9

A final tap of the judge's gavel signaled the end to months of trials and testimony. The courtroom cleared and people returned to their daily routines. The detectives now had new cases to tackle. The judges examined their dockets. Even the media had nothing new to report surrounding the events once the last Fryer was safely ensconced in the Fort Madison Penitentiary. Memories of the Gitchie Manitou murders faded from daily life and things returned to normal. Except for the families of the victims.

Sandra did her best to pick up the remnants of her former life, the one filled with television shows about happy families and excited chatter about a weekend with friends before the start of class on Monday mornings. At school, two teachers worked tirelessly to try to help her catch up on the work she'd missed over the last year and a half when she'd been away to testify at trials. But even their help wasn't enough to counteract the judgmental stares in the classrooms and the cruel whispers as girls passed her in the hallways. Hardest of all, though, was the avoidance, the leper-like status that kept many at bay. Kids at school kept their distance, not wanting to be associated with the "Gitchie Girl," a term that was now often used in place of her name.

She could have risen above the heartless comments that were said just loud enough for her to hear. And after enduring months of face-to-face encounters with the murderers, she could have brushed off the repulsive looks from the corners of sanctimonious eyes. But what tore at her soul was the isolation. The seclusion from the lunch tables. The exclusion from after-school get-togethers. Most of the mothers of her former friends no longer allowed their daughters to keep company with the tainted "Gitchie Girl," as if the violence that had been perpetrated against Sandra somehow made her a disreputable person. She wanted to hear, "There's the girl who helped put those killers behind bars." Instead, it was callous whispers. Always whispers followed by kids turning around in their seats and glancing at her with looks of revulsion, as though she were the one who'd committed the crimes. People avoided talking to her, as if her existence no longer deserved to be acknowledged.

Debbie remained a loyal friend, but she was older and had a job so Sandra wasn't able to see her very often. One day, two girls who'd been somewhat friendly before the Gitchie incident finally spoke to Sandra after school. She was caught off guard. She dared herself to hope. Maybe the gossip had worn itself out.

"I'm still your friend. I just wanted you to know that," the first girl said unexpectedly.

"We don't care what the other kids are saying, but..." The other girl looked down at the ground as if expecting Sandra to fill in the rest of her sentence.

"But what?" Sandra asked.

"It's just our moms. We can't talk to you on the phone, and you can't come over to our houses because, well, because that's what our moms said." The first girl shifted her textbooks from arm to arm and avoided eye contact.

Sandra knew she should feel elated that this was a starting point. Maybe the other kids would see that they could be friends with her too. Never one to judge, she didn't feel animosity; in fact, she understood their predicament. The three made plans to meet at a basketball game at the Sioux Falls Arena that weekend. While there, she met a nice boy from the town of Dell Rapids, South Dakota, twenty miles from where Sandra lived. Neither was allowed to make phone calls because at that time there were long distance charges involved, so they exchanged letters instead.

It was a nice arrangement that suited Sandra just fine. He wrote kind things about her, told about going to movies with his friends on the weekend, and made Sandra feel like maybe, just maybe, her life could return to normal again someday. His letters gave her something to look forward to, a brief bright spot in an otherwise dark week. On the days when an envelope arrived, she'd tear it open, and a smile would fill her face. Until one day she unfolded the paper to find disturbing news. It read, "Sandra, I'm sorry but my mom found out who I was writing to and will not let me write or talk to you anymore. Sorry." And that was it. The small bit of happiness had come to an end. It was another wound upon her heart.

At about the same time, the hassle of trying to meet Sandra secretly combined with not being allowed to be seen with her put too much of a strain on the friendship with the two girls who'd reached out to her. The friendship among them slowly fizzled out. But Sandra desperately needed to talk to someone. A nauseating dread sickened her thoughts with fear and apprehension each time she prepared to leave the safety of her house. Even the solace of her room no longer offered comfort. The emptiness of the nights filled her with the nagging feeling that something bad was about to happen. Sandra didn't realize that professional counseling was even an option, and no one offered it to her. Ever. Her own family avoided the topic of what she had lived through. Her brothers, who wanted to help their sister but weren't sure how, felt it was best for Sandra if she didn't dredge up details about "that night." It was typical of the time to simply not talk about uncomfortable topics in the belief that the pain would eventually go away on its own.

"It doesn't do any good to bring up all the ugliness."

"It's over and done with."

"It's time to move on with your life."

She wasn't even sure who'd told her those things, but she heard the platitudes each time she dared to broach the subject of "that night." She grasped at anything that would help ease the pain, including her love of music. She would climb the stairs to her room, shut out the world, and play a song by the Grassroots over and over on the record player while lying on her bed sobbing. She tried to move on, to forget about what happened. She tried to ignore the snide comments. She tried to pretend the whispers and disgusted voices weren't about her, the "Gitchie Girl."

But it was no use. She no longer fit in. Sandra felt twenty years older than the other girls. She'd grown up beyond her years while they were still able to giggle about first kisses and the school dance next weekend. But no one wanted to dance with the "Gitchie Girl." People she'd thought were her friends had disappeared. Her brother Jim went off to the Marines and Bob left for college. As soon as she was able, Sandra dropped out of school and soon after her brother Bill followed. Her downward spiral escalated.

Chapter 31

The anniversary of the murders each year was especially difficult for Sandra. She soon found that she could cope with the unbearable pain of the day by partying and drinking away the bad thoughts in the evenings with friends. It was a method she turned to when she could no longer handle the horrendous emotions that clouded her life. At fifteen Sandra was already showing classic signs of survivor's guilt and post-traumatic stress, although the diagnosis itself had not yet been coined. She still dreaded leaving the house and spent hours tucked away in her darkened bedroom with the covers pulled tight around her, crying until her mind went numb. She'd beg God to make it all go away and prayed that He could make it all be a bad dream so she could wake up and go on with her old life. Yet it seemed to her that God wasn't listening anymore. She began to grow angry with Him. How could He have let this happen?

For the past two years, she had refused to sleep unless her mom was next to her for comfort when Sandra would wake up screaming. Before bed, she'd pray to God to let her dream about Roger and the boys so she could be with them again. But those dreams never came. It was always the nightmares instead. When it seemed God did not hear her, she started to doubt and question whether there even was a God. There were blocks of time when Sandra was able to shut out the pain and to others she appeared to be functioning very well. She landed a job and performed the tasks as required. Throughout her life, she'd proved herself to be a hard worker.

Lolo was working long hours and seldom home. Her brothers for the most part were out of the house and on their own. Evenings were the worst. The daylight would fade into the darkness that frequently sent Sandra into a panic or depression. She would lie curled up on her bed and cry uncontrollably. Often, she'd turn to music to hear the comforting sound of another human voice.

Inevitably, a song would come on the radio that reminded her of Roger or one of the other boys and this would leave her devastated. She couldn't shake the feeling of lethargy that had come to control her life. Sleep would eventually enter her anguished mind only to have her startle awake in the middle of the night screaming from the relentless nightmares.

Morning, which no longer held any possibility of hope, bled into evening as she plodded through each day, having been driven to the point of emotional despair. Her eyes betrayed the dark signs of sleepless nights. Sandra trudged from bed, pulled the curtains together tighter, and crumpled back onto the mattress while waves of anxiety washed over her. She couldn't fight the hopelessness much longer. She dug her fingernails into the waning meat of her forearm to transfer her mental pain into physical pain if only for a moment.

Church bells chimed in the distance, and it occurred to Sandra that today was Sunday. She'd lost track. With every chime, she covered her ears tighter. The cheerful toll of the bells only served as a reminder that God had abandoned her. *Why? Why am I alive? Why did the boys have to die when they loved life so much? Why didn't I die with them?* But she didn't feel even a whisper of an answer. The bells chimed again. The sound filled her with a sudden fury. She bolted up in bed and threw her pillow at the wall toward the mocking sound and let out a rolling scream. "WHY? WHY? WHY? WHY?" she shouted over and over until her strength was sapped and she collapsed, once again pulling the covers over her snarled hair and feeling hot tears slide down her face in the stifling darkness.

Sandra was a survivor. It was in her nature to help, to heal, to make the world a better place whether that meant helping a struggling animal or a stranger in need. An unfamiliar feeling had begun to haunt her during these long stretches of self-imposed solitary confinement. Maybe she wasn't supposed to have lived. Maybe Allen was supposed to have killed her, too, and by some huge cosmic mistake she was still here. Maybe the only solution was...

She cut off the thought before it went any further this time. Sandra the survivor had met her challenge. She stood in the kitchen staring into an open cupboard. She removed a box of crackers, but put it back and moved on to the next cupboard. She felt she should eat but had no appetite. Finally settling on a vanilla wafer, she headed back upstairs to the bathroom, intending to brush her hair if she still had the strength by the time she got there.

Sandra stood before the mirror and gazed with disgust at her reflection. She was wearing a wrinkled, oversized T-shirt and hadn't shaven her legs in days. She pulled down the edge of one eye and recoiled at the grayish, bloodshot eyes then took a step back. Who was this pathetic stranger? When had she given up and not even realized it? Something invisible was destroying her from the inside out. No one saw it, so it was allowed to go unchecked, slowly eating away whatever parts of her it desired. The despair rendered her powerless. The life she'd once hoped for now seemed out of reach. The image in the mirror was a different Sandra. She wasn't sure if the two of them could co-exist in the same body. And again the thought that she should not be alive slipped into her mind.

Through some unseen force, Sandra found herself at the doorstep of Roger's house day after day. Roger's older brother, the one who'd driven her to the police station the morning after the murders, had taken Sandra under his wing. He understood her pain because he felt it, too. She emptied her emotions at his feet, and he never complained about it, never told her to move on. Not once did he say he was too busy or that he didn't have time to listen to her. Most days she just hung out there, feeling welcome and knowing that his family didn't blame her for what happened. That alone eased her grief. She'd play foosball with Roger's siblings. They also had a dog that Sandra adored who had been trained to take unlit cigarettes out of people's mouths because Roger's brother didn't like smoking. It was one of the few things that made Sandra laugh at the time. She discovered that when the dog was lying on her lap, a peace wafted through her. She would vigorously scratch his ears or pull his head next to hers and sing winsome songs softly into his ears. The dog never tired of the attention, of course, and Sandra longed for a dog of her own.

Roger's mother was supportive even though her own pain was excruciating. For almost a year, Sandra would arrive at their house nearly every day feeling that life was unbearable. His family had crutched her through each day, and she knew that without them she couldn't have found the strength to go on. But the strain of losing a son in such a horrible manner took its toll on Roger's mother, too. By the year's end, she passed away. Sandra, along with the Essem family, was devastated. Soon after that, the Essem family began to head in different directions. They were older now, getting married and moving off on their own. The security she'd once had in their home had run its course.

Chapter 32

An indescribable hurt returned that festered inside Sandra, spreading to her edges and forming to the shape of her body like a toxic gas inside a bottle. She couldn't escape the emotional pain. And if she somehow managed to erase the garbled memories through partying and alcohol, it simply rippled back during her sickened slumber and she awoke to a fresh round of anguish. Her instinct for survival was so fierce that she tried various methods to right her life again. When she had nowhere else to put the pain, she would go to Roger's grave and sing to him. She'd let the words and rhythms gently shake the worst of the hurt from the weary fibers of her body.

It was her season of loneliness. Lolo and her brothers, though largely absent for most of the day, loved Sandra. Her grandparents were dead, no one had heard from her father in years, friends had abandoned her. Yet when she thought of Roger and the perfect times they'd spent together, she felt a glimmer of hope that she could reclaim her life again someday. So she clung to his memory, sang to him, and let him know that he would live on forever in a special corner of her mind. And with this one optimistic thought, she cut away a sliver of the pain, allowing her to smooth its rough edges. It was a start. She kept Roger safe in her mind. She'd never again feel the tender kisses he'd once placed on her lips, but she felt his spirit whenever she succeeded in pushing the ugly emotions to the side through melody and music before the awful feelings returned and knocked her down as if hit by a loaded spring unleashed with a vengeance.

"Come shopping with me," Debbie said, making a point of sounding upbeat. She was worried about Sandra. It had been two years since the murders at Gitchie Manitou, and she was never certain whether she'd call and discover that Sandra was in another one of her "dark" moods.

"No, I'm going to Roger's grave." She didn't say it with any expectation of empathy. It was just a fact, and she wasn't ashamed or embarrassed to let anyone know about one of the few things that relieved her pain. "There was a song on the radio this morning that reminded me of him, and I just want to sing to him." It was true. For some reason the moment she'd heard the song it had reminded her of the day the two of them spent at Falls Park, his arm around her waist, her head on his shoulder. For whatever reason, she couldn't get Roger out of her head today.

Debbie paused and twisted the phone cord around her finger. Her heart had broken for Sandra so many times since Roger had died. "Sandra, I'm just wondering...it's just a thought. Um, do you think it might be better if you didn't go? You know, maybe it's harder to keep thinking about Roger, and if you just moved on..." Debbie knew Sandra still loved him but worried that her friend was holding onto a ghost out of guilt perhaps.

Sandra looked up at the ceiling and let out a sigh. She wasn't mad at Debbie. It was just that no one seemed to understand. She couldn't forget Roger. She couldn't forget any of them, and she especially couldn't forget that night. She tried, but the memories were right there, dancing at the corner of every thought. "I know everyone thinks that, but you don't understand. When I go to his grave, I feel him. I mean I really feel *him*. Maybe it's not like feeling his arms around me, but it's like he knows I'm there. Like he can see me."

She would talk to Roger. She confessed to him that she didn't think she'd ever actually told him her age. She'd meant to after their first date. And once when Roger had come to pick her up she'd introduced him to Debbie and her sister. After a hurried conversation, it seemed he was left with the impression that Sandra was in the same grade as Debbie, who was actually three years older, rather than the intended message that they both went to school in Harrisburg. Sandra had let it slide, and then it just never came up again before the fateful night.

So she did go and sit by his grave for hours, singing to him and pleading with him to understand that he and the other boys were her heroes.

"We didn't even get to say goodbye before you were gone. And in spite of terrible pain Mike and Stew remained strong. I think even Dana, who was so young, knew things were worse than I thought. You are my heroes, and I never had the chance to tell you."

She talked and sang until finally the burden of pain lifted from her shoulders slightly. For the rest of the day, she waited for the horrible feelings to come back, but that didn't happen. Instead, a strange sensation, as if a layer of pain had been rinsed away, left her with clarity and freshness, unfamiliar feelings that she hadn't experienced for a long time. She felt almost, well, normal again.

She'd managed to push the darkness away but only for the time being. Sandra had gone back to a job during the day. Debbie worked at a truck stop just off the interstate that was close to both of their houses. The minimum age for employment there was sixteen, and Sandra was only fifteen, so she and Debbie cleverly modified Sandra's birth certificate so she'd appear to be sixteen. Working gave Sandra an escape from the uncontrollable sadness that tainted her life. The job distracted her for hours at a time, allowing some semblance of a normal life to return.

When Debbie called a few days later, Sandra went with her to a party.

"I don't know a lot of these people," Sandra said, looking around at the crowd after they'd arrived at the house where one of Debbie's co-workers lived. The house was a sprawling ranch style, every room packed elbow-to-elbow with partygoers, and music pulsed through the house from oversized speakers. It wasn't long before a clean-cut boy in a button-down shirt handed Sandra and Debbie each a beer. In the kitchen, people crowded around a Formica table telling stories and roaring with laughter. The door to the gold-colored refrigerator was working overtime with people helping themselves to the well-stocked shelves of beer.

Sandra gravitated to the living room and settled onto a long, armless couch. "Let's sit here. I don't feel so claustrophobic," she told Debbie. Sandra liked this atmosphere where no one made the connection she was *that girl*. The "Gitchie Girl." She still heard the reference occasionally. She knew her brothers did, too, though they never let on to Sandra about it. A friend had told her this after too many beers one night. Sandra tried not to worry much about what others thought of her. There was nothing she could do now to change that night. The beer she'd been sipping had gone warm, but she didn't want to give up her coveted spot on the couch

"Sandra!" The person yelled her name with such enthusiasm she thought it must be an old friend. It wasn't. It was a boy she didn't recognize but remembered meeting through a friend after he said his name.

"Remember me? That was quite the night," he said as if there were a period between each word. He seemed vaguely familiar. Memories of that night had been fuzzy at the time and even more so now. She was reluctant to admit to herself that it had been harder to concentrate and focus since the whole ordeal with the murders, especially when it came to meeting new people. It was as if her mind had formed a protective barrier between itself and anything unknown. This boy had lively eyes and an engaging smile. Did he seem trustworthy or was it just that she missed her old life? The one where she'd attracted friends so easily that she'd broken through to the popular crowds with practically no effort. Perhaps it just felt good to hear someone shouting her name, seeking her out as if she were the life of the party. For whatever reason, Sandra nodded and smiled. He was friendly and there was no one else to talk to. Before the night was over, the new friend had given her a handful of pills, "white cross" he called them, along with his phone number in case she wanted more.

She never did call him. However, Sandra began regularly drinking beer with a group of people who liked to party. She acquired a daily routine that passed for a normal life to the casual observer. But then the depression would descend without warning, and her balance would sink away as if it had been resting on quicksand the whole time. One day she was thankful to God for saving her life at Gitchie and the next wishing He wouldn't have.

Sandra's life remained derailed. The tragedy at Gitchie Manitou had thrown her into a world foreign to most teenagers. She'd dropped out of school, was working full-time, and had moved into an apartment in Sioux Falls with her brother Bill. She was basically a sixteen-year-old adult. A new job came her way at Raven Industries, a factory where she sewed clothes, something she'd always loved doing in home economics class at school. Sandra liked the simple things in life: sewing, spending time with family, and music. Her life was simple but predictable. She occupied her mind with work during the day and often numbed her mind with beer and partying during the night. It kept all the bad stuff at bay temporarily.

She didn't want to start drinking alone, so she and some friends would gather at one of their houses in the evenings to drink and listen to rock music. Always the music. Sandra loved music and dancing, and one night found herself dancing with a young man who soon became her boyfriend. Neither of them wanted to admit that they fueled each other in a bad way. Somehow they each ended up with a bag of white cross pills. Sandra hadn't even thought of the pills since that party months ago when she'd been given her first one. There were a hundred pills, and she took them regularly, washing down a couple in the morning with a glass of juice and then not needing to eat again until evening. It was speed, someone had told her, and the energy kept her going all day, but she crashed at night. She lost ten pounds she didn't need to lose, but it was nothing that made her feel fantastic. When the pills ran out, she never felt the desire to take them again. The days of pills were over.

But when the Gitchie Manitou demons came back to haunt her, she still had the comfort of her drinking buddies. There were times when she thought life was getting back to normal and mornings when she could hardly muster the energy to get out of bed. It felt as if all the joy had been sucked out of her life and there was no point in moving on. She dreaded the month of November as the calendar steadily crept toward the seventeenth, the anniversary of the murders. She wanted to talk about what had happened so desperately, but it seemed that even her family avoided the topic, not knowing what to say. She never received a card or phone call. She wanted to know that someone understood her pain, but she'd inevitably spend that day alone, and it seemed as if time stood still. She wanted someone to love her despair away. She wanted a normal life. She wanted...someone.

A series of on-again, off-again relationships followed. She came home after work one evening to find that a neighbor's party had spilled onto the back porch. Sandra joined them and before the night was over had met a strong, good-looking man with long, dark hair who would first become her boyfriend and later a lifelong friend. They just couldn't get on the same wavelength, and when they were together they drank too much. He eventually moved away.

With a strong sense of loyalty, Sandra rarely parted ways harshly with anyone. Over the next few years she would meet several boyfriends who would stay in touch with her. The relationships were often toxic and short-lived. Sandra's desire for love and stability was intense. She latched onto others for support, but that one person who could not only give but accept love and accept her past eluded her. If only she could find that person, she knew she could rebuild her life. More time passed, however, and the security she desperately craved seemed as though it would never happen.

She couldn't find the key to letting go and moving on, though it seemed she tried everything to make the pain go away. One evening Bill returned to the apartment and found her perched on the edge of the couch with India ink and a needle. She'd tattooed a large "RO" on her upper arm and was preparing to add the "GER." It was the only way she could think of to show that she hadn't forgotten Roger. It would tie a piece of him to her forever. Bill threw the ink in the garbage and returned to console Sandra. "No, sis, you don't want to do that."

Chapter 33

Just before turning eighteen, Sandra moved to a small town in Minnesota with Bill's girlfriend, who was attending an interior design school there. The two girls lived in a cozy loft-style apartment above the design school, and Sandra got a job in a retail store downtown. It was a relief living in this town where no one knew of her past. There were no sideways glances followed by the look of *aha* when they realized who she was. The "Gitchie Girl." It was a fresh start in this new town, but she missed her family and everything that was familiar.

Toward the end of the school year, the two of them went back to Sioux Falls to find places to live since their stint in Minnesota was nearly over. Sandra went out with two of her brothers to a popular pub downtown. While there, she was introduced to her brother's boss, Carroll Chrans, who owned a pawnshop next to the pub. Carroll offered Sandra a job but needed her to start immediately. Sandra hadn't moved back from Minnesota yet, so she had to decline the job offer. She didn't realize how fateful that night would become.

Upon Sandra's return, she and Bill moved into a dingy apartment on the outskirts of Sioux Falls that was conveniently just down the street from her old friend Debbie. The apartment was so bare that in December her brother Jim showed up with a Christmas tree because he felt horrible about their living conditions and thought everyone should at least have a tree. The greenery brought cheer to the otherwise dismal furnishings, yet she was simply relieved to have a steady job, a place to live, and a family who cared so much about her.

She worked at a retail store for a while and later at the mall. All around her, friends and relatives were getting married and building happy lives. Sandra continued to search for someone to love, but all she found was disappointment. A series of failed and dysfunctional relationships filled the years with their empty promises taunting her with the prospect of affection which remained just beyond her grasp.

After one frenzied relationship fizzled out, she refused to mope in her apartment and decided to visit a friend. On the way there, she cranked the music and roared down the interstate, hoping her junker car wouldn't give out. Dusk was approaching, so she flipped on the headlights and spotted a small mound on the road just ahead. She hit the brakes, steered the car to the shoulder, and craned her neck, glancing out the window to see what she'd almost hit. When she saw what it was, she felt a pang in her heart. Sandra shifted into park, got out, walked over to what had caught her eye, and found it was a small turtle that had probably strayed from a nearby pond. Its curious eyes looked at her as she returned it to the grassy ditch. "You better stay off that highway," she scolded the little guy. It's strange, she thought smiling, how one disoriented turtle can bring joy to an otherwise worthless day.

Years went by and Sandra couldn't find her footing in life or love. She'd tried partying away her problems, tried pills, tried building a life with different men, even tried moving to Minnesota. Nothing had helped. Her bouts of anger at God continued. To top it off, she now lived in a dilapidated house with two of her brothers. At least they could lean on one another, but Sandra felt ungrounded, like a weightless feather at the mercy of whichever wind decided to toss her here or there. How much disorder could she endure? Yet she never gave up hope of finding that perfect relationship. Not perfect actually, she wasn't that starry-eyed, but perfect for her. Somewhere there had to be the right guy to build a happy life with. That man was closer than she knew, and she'd already met him.

Chapter 34

"For I know the plans I have for you," declares the LORD, "plans for welfare and not for evil, to give you a future and a hope."

Jeremiah 29:11 (ESV)

Months blended into years while Sandra continued the unsatisfying chorus in her life of moving from one half-respectable apartment to another, finding a promising boyfriend only to have the relationship fall apart, and changing jobs just as often. She was in her mid-twenties and worried that the happily-ever-after she so fiercely sought might forever elude her. *Haven't I met you more than halfway?* she reasoned with God. I've tried to be a good person. Her relationship with God seemed to be as fluctuating as the rest of her life. It wasn't that she expected the perfect house with the white picket fence; she just wanted a shot at a normal life with a man who could love and respect her the way she so deeply desired. Trying to keep an optimistic attitude, she added a postscript to her prayers. *I'm so thankful I've never been in a physically abusive relationship; not with my dad, or any of my boyfriends.* She looked on that as a blessing from God.

Sandra's current job as a waitress at The Cantina in the mall had been a blessing as well. The tip money was good, so perhaps she and her brother Bill would be able to move into a better apartment soon. Right now, her feet ached and her back hurt. It had been a long shift, but at least there was a lull.

No sooner had she sat down than she heard a customer come in through the front door. She looked up to find Carroll Chrans, her brother's boss, whom she'd known on a casual basis for some time now. He ordered one beer, they talked for a while, and then Carroll left but came back several more times over the course of the month when the place just happened to be empty.

It seemed a little odd to Sandra that he usually ordered only one beer, but odd in a good way. She couldn't count many people she knew who generally stopped after one beer, including herself. And that wasn't the only thing she noticed during their increasingly frequent conversations. Carroll was kind and polite. He talked about his mother and family. He didn't have rough edges or a restless spirit. He was content and confident. He had goals. So when he finally asked her out on a date, she accepted.

Everything with Carroll seemed different, a good kind of different. But Sandra wasn't used to the good part and found it to be an acquired taste. Carroll didn't take her to wild parties and loud bars, her familiar standbys. Instead, they went to movies like *Back to the Future* and *The Jewel of the Nile* followed by a late-night snack at Perkins; a salad for Sandra and a hamburger for Carroll eaten over a leisurely conversation about life and family. For both of them, the conversations always came back to family.

Sandra's intuitiveness brought out the best in Carroll as well. With her patient ways, those around her felt comfortable, so he shared the intimate parts of his life with ease.

"I grew up in Rapid City, but when Dad ended up in a hospital near Sioux Falls I hitchhiked three hundred and sixty-five miles across the state to get here because I had no car and little money." He let out a soft chuckle and gave his head a reminiscent shake. "I actually slept on park benches! I didn't care though. My only focus was getting to Dad so I could take care of him." Carroll told the story with such flourish that by the time he finished it was nearly 1:00 AM.

"Please don't tell me you're still getting up in the morning at six o'clock to get that paperwork done before you open the shop," Sandra said, and Carroll nodded that he was. Thinking of her typical daily routine Sandra added, "You might be the first person I've dated who doesn't usually party all night and get up in the middle of the afternoon to get ready for work!"

He wouldn't have considered sleeping in when there was work to be done. Carroll still owned the pawnshop that Sandra's brother had worked at for several years. After arriving in Sioux Falls to care for his dad, he had rented a rather squalid store next to a tavern in a strip of old brick buildings just off of downtown and started the first pawnshop in the city. He rose early, worked long hours, and ended the day by taking Sandra on a date nearly every night of the week. She wasn't sure how much money he made, but based on the simplicity of their dates, she assumed it wasn't much. For Sandra, money wasn't even a consideration. This was about a relationship. Their dates continued to be modest, finding out-of-the-way places to talk or watching television at home over a bowl of popcorn. One Saturday Sandra awoke mid-morning feeling refreshed and not missing the blahs that came after a night of partying into the wee hours. Perhaps Carroll's method of "work hard, unwind, sleep, repeat" wasn't so bad.

It wasn't just his relentless drive that surprised her; it was his unfailing kindness almost to a fault. As the two of them sat watching a late movie at home, Sandra knew something was amiss. "What's going on? You seem really distracted." This was unusual for Carroll, who readily pushed work aside when it was "their time" to focus on the two of them.

Finally Carroll confessed there was a problem brewing that had hijacked his thoughts. "Two years ago I caught an employee stealing from the shop. When I asked him why, I discovered he was paying medical bills due to his child's ongoing health problems and his car was in the shop until he paid the mechanic. He came clean, so I figured he deserved a second chance." The raucous laugh track of the TV in the background distracted Sandra from his story, and she simultaneously fumbled for the remote while moving closer to Carroll. Right now, he was all that mattered. She clicked the TV off. "A month ago I caught him stealing again, but only because his rent was overdue, and he'd had every intention of replacing the money with his next check. I'm not a pushover, but the guy's almost like family to me, and sometimes compassion is more important than a buck. So I gave him the benefit of the doubt again only to discover today that he hadn't rung up a sale."

Sandra was stunned. She'd never known anyone with that much faith in another human before. Perhaps if Carroll were capable of forgiving and accepting someone so deeply, there was hope he'd accept her faults as well. They talked into the early morning hours until Carroll, with logical thinking and infinite patience, determined a course of action regarding the employee. The man would get one final chance but would never have access to the cash register again. Sandra's respect for Carroll surged, and she now had eyes for no one else.

Chapter 35
February 1986

"I'M GETTING MARRIED," Sandra shouted into the phone, laughing. After a year of dating, Carroll had proposed at the end of a long night, and the first thing Sandra did was call Lolo.

"Call me back later, and we'll make some plans," Lolo mumbled, half asleep.

When Sandra called back, Lolo was already up and waiting for the call so she could take her to the mall. The two of them picked out the prettiest dress they could find and together packed Sandra's suitcase. Carroll had purchased last-minute plane tickets, and by the next day he and Sandra were headed to Las Vegas, where they were married in the Little White Chapel. It hadn't sunk in yet that everything she'd wanted for all these years now lay before her like a lavish feast. The only thing missing from her wedding, she surmised, was the fact that her brothers and Lolo hadn't been there. But in her heart they were all there on this special day of love.

Almost immediately upon returning home, Sandra and Carroll set off on a month-long honeymoon, driving down Highway 101 in California and even stopping to see his sister. Sandra made her first foray into the ocean, wandered among giant Redwoods, and fell in love with traveling. To pass the time during the long car rides, they would pepper each other with questions.

"Will you stay married to me if I go broke?" he asked, somewhat seriously.

"Yes," and she meant it. When she married him, it had been because she wanted, needed, and couldn't live without his deep love.

"If I go bald?"

"Yes."

"Lose my teeth and need dentures?"

"Yes!"

"Gain so much weight you have to roll me over to the shop every day?"

"Yes!" They were both laughing by now, and Sandra kept reminding him to watch the road, but he already was. The questioning continued until he finally came up with the golden question.

"What if I became a pig farmer?"

"Okay, then, NO! That's where I draw the line, even though I love piglets," she laughed, recalling the summertime stench of a relative's pig farm. Though truthfully, she'd have been right beside him slopping the hogs.

The honeymoon itself ended, but their feelings for each other grew. Carroll worked long hours every day to build up the pawnshop along with two fireworks stands he'd started a few years ago in a nearby town. The pawnshop outgrew its old space, and they took a chance on a more expensive one-year lease of a large shop that became profitable overnight. The place was so successful that within months they were house shopping.

"Oh, Carroll! It's like a Terry Redland painting," Sandra gasped when she first saw the sprawling house on an acre of wooded land. They moved into the dream house, but in typical Carroll fashion, he had made sure they still had plenty of money to help others.

"How much do you owe your mom?" he asked Sandra before the ink on their mortgage had dried, knowing that Lolo was the one who'd helped Sandra numerous times over the years when she was between jobs or needed help with a car payment. When Sandra told him the amount, he made a plan to pay Lolo back as well.

Sandra adored Carroll's two boys, Joshua, six, and Jacob, four, from Carroll's first marriage that hadn't worked out. So when the boys came to stay on weekends, Sandra forged bonds with her new sons who completed her life, while Carroll worked the small firecracker stands and pawnshop. She made a commitment to treat them like her own, and one night when Jacob sat in the bathtub with shampoo piled on his head, he turned to her and asked, "Sandra, did you lay me?"

"What do you mean?" she asked while perched on the edge of the tub, reaching for the basket of toys she'd already compiled for the boys.

"You know, like a chicken lays a egg. Did you lay me in a egg?"

Sandra laughed until her sides hurt but at the same time marveled at how close she and the boys had become in such a short time. Her family had grown. Besides Carroll and their sons, Sandra had also been blessed with two half-brothers, Jeff and Jason, and a half-sister over the years although she never considered them "half." They were family, and to Sandra family meant love.

Every summer shortly after the fireworks stands closed down for the year, the four of them would embark on a month-long vacation. The first stop was usually the other side of the state where Carroll's mom lived. All of them would pitch in to help with work around her house, Carroll undertaking some major job like repairing the water cistern while the boys picked up sticks in the yard. But after that, the real fun began, and they were off to Disneyland or South Padre Island, where Carroll astounded them by renting a condo right on the beach and immersing the boys in all the experiences a summer vacation could offer. He worked hard during the year and made sure that his time away from work was well spent, splurging and showering his family with surprises. They traveled to Maui, taking both of their mothers with them. One spring, Carroll and Sandra headed to a Sandals Resort in the Caribbean, and he reserved a small bus just for them so they could spend time as a couple. Another year they traveled to the jewelry mart in downtown Los Angeles, where they spent tens of thousands of dollars for store inventory, and Sandra quickly developed a talent for spotting what would appeal to their customers.

Then there were the Christmases where he lavished Sandra with jewelry and one time fifteen bottles of perfume from Macy's. On several occasions, he drove through a run-down neighborhood and threw money out the window in hopes that a person in need would find it. Sandra, who'd never even looked at the checkbook since the day they were married, wasn't surprised when he showed up with a new car for their son Joshua when he turned sixteen.

He wasn't just generous with his immediate family. His mom's birthday was July third, so every year after the Fourth of July sales were over, he closed the stands, which he'd now built into two giant warehouses and three fireworks stores. Dozens of friends and family would get together in a nearby resort town, where Carroll rented a block of rooms and put on a birthday party for his mom. No one in the group would drink and drive, and Carroll realized the limo was costing him so much money that he'd be better off buying one. Which he did.

"He's the only person I know who can make a seventy-year-old lady feel like the prettiest woman on earth," his mom said after concluding her tenth limo ride of the weekend. Almost as soon as one ride was over she would cluck with surprise at herself that she'd forgotten to pick up some small item, which would then require yet another limo ride to retrieve it.

During these peaceful moments, happiness seeped into Sandra and acted like a salve on the Gitchie Manitou scars that still marred her spirit. The scars faded to a lighter hue, but they didn't go away completely. Having a family and a routine kept her balanced. She and Carroll worked together, went to lunch together, and after work would go out for a beer, something that he had done since he'd started his first business. Occasionally the detectives from Iowa would stop by the pawnshop just to talk and see how she was doing. Most days were good, but there were still bad days, and during one of these bouts she found herself praying the Lord's Prayer over and over, waiting to get to the line about "deliver us from evil," which gave her a peace that passed understanding. She went to church a few times, but it was as if her self-esteem only held up in familiar surroundings. Inside the church she felt unworthy, like a stain of a person dirtying up the sanctuary. She went to church with Carroll's mom, with her own mom, and with her son Jacob, but she felt like an outcast, never comfortable. In the silence of her home, she'd reach out to God with simple heartfelt prayers that were sometimes answered in ways she didn't expect.

Today was one of those bad days. Some business problems had cropped up in the past weeks. To top it off, a relative had unknowingly mentioned something that pulled the murders to the front of her mind. Her head pounded, her stomach sickened with the vivid memories that had flooded back. She forced herself to push forward and carry on as usual. Try to regain some order in her life. As usual, Carroll had headed for work prior to Sandra, who was getting the boys off to school before spending some time spoiling her miniature pinschers.

"Sorry, pups!" she said, quickly giving their ears a vigorous rub before answering the phone that had interrupted the morning pampering. It was her mom calling to give her an update on an abused stray dog that had been rescued from the reservation months ago. The dog, one of the dozens of strays in the area, had been following Sandra's brother Bill back and forth to work every day and would wait outside until his shift was over. Bill named him Buddy. One day, two dogs attacked Bill and Buddy leaped to his defense. Fur flew, saliva spewed, and dust rose from the ground as the dogs grappled for control with snarls and snapping teeth. Two against one placed Buddy at an unfair advantage, yet he refused to quit until Bill was safe. When it ended, Buddy lay exhausted and bleeding in the dirt. Bill rushed him home and with the help of Lolo and his brother Jeff dressed the open wounds, including a deep gash that had sliced Buddy's throat. It didn't look like he'd make it.

Later, the vet determined Buddy had been shot and his back leg broken at some point during his life. He had splotches of bare skin from mange, his breathing was labored, bones stuck out from his ribs, his ear was nearly torn in half, and bandages covered the sores and bites that riddled his body. After a long recovery, Buddy was up and running, and he'd greet his family with blinking eyes and a quaking tail every morning, but Lolo, in spite of her big heart, had a fear of dogs.

So of course, Sandra took Buddy as her rescue project and began intensive support to heal his emotional scars. In spite of his past, Buddy never snarled and even let her other dogs take the special treats from his dish. What Sandra noticed that first day was that every time she reached out to comfort him, a piece of her discontent slipped away. By evening, the memories of Gitchie had faded to the background where they belonged. While the business problems still remained, she and Carroll had set a plan, and she had the strength to move forward. They'd closed the fireworks stands due to fierce competition from similar businesses, and as business goes, the pawnshops were on a downswing as well. Both agreed the important thing was that they had each other and family.

Years later when she first saw the term "pet therapy," Sandra realized how many animals had been put in her path over the years to help her through her own troubles: she would place crickets in a cup to release outside, help birds with broken wings, and check the paper every morning to see if there were any ads for lost animals she might recognize. The seed had been planted. Instead of conjuring up the awful memories that had consumed her thoughts that morning, she recalled the times she'd told her grandpa that she wanted to save all the animals in the world and bring them to his farm.

At the time she hadn't realized how big the world was or how ugly it could seem at times, but as she stroked Buddy's bristly head the thought occurred to her that maybe, just maybe, it wasn't a mistake that she'd survived that night. Maybe, she allowed herself to think, maybe she had a purpose for being here. Buddy had been broken, abused, cast out and frightened but never gave up. Tears rolled down Sandra's cheeks, and suddenly she was next to him on the floor, her head next to his, sobbing uncontrollably and trying to forget that night long ago when her life had seemed as hopeless as his once had. Sandra had discovered pet therapy on her own and helping animals would become an ongoing part of her life. On her dream board, a bulletin board covered with all the things she hoped to see and do someday, she posted a note: *Open my own no-kill animal rescue shelter.*

Life is a journey consisting of many paths. Some we choose. Some are chosen for us. Sandra had Carroll and the boys to accompany her on this journey now, and they'd wisely chosen paths lined with blessings. Yet she continued to sense that something wicked lingered nearby, and this wickedness, whatever it was, repeatedly slithered back into her life when she least expected it. Even when it was silent she always knew it was there, just beyond the darkness of the tree line. The evil had never quite left her completely, though over the years she'd tried various ways to escape it and was now preparing to triumph over it.

The girl who had demonstrated resilience repeatedly showed her grit again more than four decades after the murders when she arranged what she would later describe as an event that felt like an encounter between good and evil. On a hot spring day, Sandra traveled to Iowa's Fort Madison, a maximum security prison, for a face-to-face meeting with Allen Fryer, "the Boss." David and James both refused her request for a meeting. She had prepared a list of questions, yet these weren't the primary reason for the visit. That she would explain to Allen later in the day. Yet prior to the meeting, years of pent-up emotions surfaced into physical symptoms that nearly caused the trip to be cancelled. For days Sandra had been plagued with relentless nausea, fever, weakness, and insomnia. She collapsed from exhaustion just before embarking on the journey to the prison, but was able to remain strong enough to continue.

Sunlight glistened off the razor sharp rolls of concertina wire high atop the looming walls of the prison. Behind these walls live some of society's most dangerous and violent inmates. And into this atmosphere rife with despondency, Sandra finally stood.

Clank! Slam! The sounds of incarceration echoed in the empty hallway from where she'd just come and which was now separated from the visitation room, where she stood by an industrial steel door. Beneath the bright glare of the fluorescent light with its faint hum, she stood trembling and overcome with emotion. In the brief moments before Allen entered the room Sandra silently prayed, *God, please give me strength to proceed with what needs to be said.* And then for the first time in days, her anxiety immediately slipped away, replaced by the glow of confidence.

Allen sat down wordlessly, his face drawn and hard from years of life on the inside; he was directly in front of her, and to her side stood a prison guard for her protection. Sandra started by thanking him for the meeting, since the brothers had rejected nearly all interview requests over the past four decades. Then she confronted him about shooting Roger, but he denied doing this and in fact denied shooting anyone. Undeterred, she reminded him she had been standing next to Mike when Allen shot him. Allen denied it and claimed it must have been one of his brothers. Realizing where this was headed, Sandra switched course and asked him what he would have done differently. He said he'd change nothing because his brothers had wanted to kill her, but he had saved her.

The room fell silent with only the din of fluorescent lights humming above.

"Why didn't you kill me?"

He replied it was because she had reminded him of his stepdaughter who was about the same age. Then Sandra told him he had done the right thing by not killing her; she was able to go on and experience life. This had been her primary purpose for facing Allen. They shook hands. The meeting was over, and so was the confrontation Sandra had long anticipated. Later, she would tell people it felt as if a thousand pounds had been lifted off her. Outside the prison she noticed that even the colors seemed brighter, the grass greener, the sky bluer, and the sun felt warmer. Sandra had reached another goal in her healing process.

With a desire to know more about her Native bloodlines, Sandra also began learning the Lakota traditions from her cousin, who has been a spiritual leader for over thirty years. It was eventually decided that he'd perform a Wiping of the Tears ceremony at Gitchie Manitou, or "Great Spirit," a sacred place to help Sandra move on even though she will never forget. Part of the Native way is to have a deep understanding before communing with nature, so Sandra began many preceremony preparations, including smudging with sage for positive feelings and to purify her surroundings. She had been told that during the ritual Roger, Mike, Stew, and Dana in the spirit world could witness this sacred event and be with her.

On the day of the healing, her cousin will wear his traditional dress, tie his long black braids with bits of cloth, and prepare the herbs—bear root, gum weed, sweet grass, and sage. A bearskin robe will be draped around Sandra's shoulders. With Native tongues chanting song and prayer, wisps of gray-tinged smoke will rise to carry the words skyward. In a strong, steady voice this spiritual leader will perform the Wiping of the Tears ceremony. He'll burn sage and place sacred tobacco at each spot where the boys' bodies had lain. At the ceremony's conclusion, Sandra's soul will be refreshed and ready to move on. She believes that her Christian faith coexists in harmony with her Native spiritual beliefs. Both have been instrumental in her continued healing.

Through philosophical discussions with Carroll and others, watching television shows about religion, and reading passages from the Bible, Sandra began to view life in a new light. She realized that God does not allow horrible things to just happen. There is conflict between good and evil in the world and sometimes evil wins the battles, as it did at Gitchie Manitou so many years ago. But evil loses the war in the end as Christ, love, and goodness prevail. Forgiveness can be hard, but forgiveness can also be powerful.

Marian Baade, mother of Dana and Stew, amazed her friends and family when she forgave the Fryer brothers for their horrendous actions, feeling that forgiveness was vital to her Christian beliefs. She passed away with peace in her heart.

On a warm spring morning Sandra and Carroll strolled through a park near their home. As they walked along holding hands, the sweet smell of lilacs drifted in the air, and robins hopped about searching for their morning breakfast. In the distance, the chiming of church bells brought a smile to Sandra's face. God is not silent; He was calling to her again, and she was listening.

She continued to build her life around the love of God, family, and friends, and in the process discovered many paths to happiness. She moved on to become Sandra the wife. Sandra the mother. Sandra the grandmother. And Sandra the caregiver who rescues animals. She couldn't change the past, so instead she'd changed her future. She was no longer "the Gitchie Girl."

Rebuilding her life and surrounded by love. Sandra with husband, Carroll, sons Jacob (left) and Joshua (right), and dog Roscoe.

As twilight settles over Gitchie Manitou casting long shadows on the aged stones and the silver sky begins to fade to dusk, the park is silent except for the chatter of small animals or the rustle of leaves as a light wind sends them scattering across gravel. Deer foraging in the tall prairie grasses lift their heads at these soft sounds, then return to their evening meal. Beyond the remains of a stone campsite, shimmering water rolls along below a steep bank. This beautiful park is now a place of peace and solitude. It is also a place where the hopes and dreams of four teenagers remain for eternity. It is a place where a young girl lost her innocence and adolescent love. Yet, it is also a place where God gave that girl strength to know that the world can be good and the courage to go on to dream new dreams. Love sustains. And God prevailed to allow her to build a life surrounded by friends and a loving family, and this love will endure forever.

About the Authors

SANDY HAMMAN has been a teacher with the Sioux City Community School District in Iowa since 1994. She specializes in teaching writing and reading.

PHIL HAMMAN started teaching in the Sioux City School District in 1986. He co-teaches high school English. He has a personal connection to the story. Mike Hadrath was Phil's best friend, and they were teammates in basketball and baseball.

Phil and Sandy have been married since 1984.

30903866R00093

Made in the USA
Middletown, DE
11 April 2016